About Island Press

Since 1984, the nonprofit organization Island Press has been stimulating, shaping, and communicating ideas that are essential for solving environmental problems worldwide. With more than 1,000 titles in print and some 30 new releases each year, we are the nation's leading publisher on environmental issues. We identify innovative thinkers and emerging trends in the environmental field. We work with world-renowned experts and authors to develop cross-disciplinary solutions to environmental challenges.

Island Press designs and executes educational campaigns, in conjunction with our authors, to communicate their critical messages in print, in person, and online using the latest technologies, innovative programs, and the media. Our goal is to reach targeted audiences—scientists, policy makers, environmental advocates, urban planners, the media, and concerned citizens—with information that can be used to create the framework for long-term ecological health and human well-being.

Island Press gratefully acknowledges major support from The Bobolink Foundation, Caldera Foundation, The Curtis and Edith Munson Foundation, The Forrest C. and Frances H. Lattner Foundation, The JPB Foundation, The Kresge Foundation, The Summit Charitable Foundation, Inc., and many other generous organizations and individuals.

The opinions expressed in this book are those of the author(s) and do not necessarily reflect the views of our supporters.

Urbanism Without Effort

Urbanism Without Effort

Reconnecting with First Principles of the City

Text and Photographs by

Charles R. Wolfe

ISLANDPRESS

Washington | Covelo | London

Library of Congress Control Number: 2018946761

All Island Press books are printed on environmentally responsible materials.

Manufactured in the United States of America
10 9 8 7 6 5 4 3 2 1

All links verified as of March 7, 2018.
Cover design by Maureen Gately.
Cover image and interior images by Charles R. Wolfe, except where otherwise noted.

Generous support for the publication of this book was provided by The Centre for the Future of Places, KTH Royal Institute of Technology.

THE CENTRE FOR THE FUTURE OF PLACES

KTH VETENSKAP OCH KONST

Keywords: Barcelona, bicycle, Campo de' Fiori, city, Cortona, Croatia, density, Diocletian's Palace, Florence, health, Jane Jacobs, Karatu, Lisbon, Maasai, Madrid, Matera, Melbourne, mobility, Ngorongoro, placemaking, Portland, Sarah Marder, Seattle, urban planning, Venice, walkability

To my father, Professor M. R. Wolfe, 1918–1989,
who taught me how to notice whole places as artifacts,
and to photograph them with care

Contents

Preface to the Revised Edition

Since the original e-book publication of *Urbanism Without Effort* over five years ago, the pace and complexity of urban change have underscored the importance of the book's original purpose: to efficiently discuss clear principles behind inviting, authentic urban environments where people feel at home.

Popular discussion of center city redevelopment and innovation has also evolved over the past five years, bringing increased attention to many significant issues. They include the role of the technology sector in urban redevelopment, the consequential impacts of gentrification, rising housing costs, homelessness, and the need for citizen empowerment. Books such as Richard Florida's *New Urban Crisis* now address the unforeseen symptoms of urban resilience movements and assess the viability of prior, broad-based assumptions of urban prosperity. Simultaneously, global movements based on the United Nations New Urban Agenda focus on an equity-based call for implementation of the "City We Need."

Unfortunately, this popular discussion—while increasingly widespread in scope—is often compromised by cursory social media and the rapid information turnover of daily news cycles. Hence, as in 2013, I believe that a more reflective understanding of precedent should guide today's discussions about city life.

While many people lament the loss of authentic places, or endlessly debate the now commonly known economic and political pitfalls of today's urban redevelopment, it is important to first remember the roles of inspiration, historical context, and space-based cues in framing the sustainable, inviting urban environments that we all seek.

While my 2017 companion book, *Seeing the Better City*, provides considerable guidance on how to critically observe and understand these environments, it also spurred many expressions of interest in an updated edition of *Urbanism Without Effort* in paperback and revised e-book formats. With the encouragement and support of Dr. Tigran Haas and the Centre for the Future of Places at KTH University in Stockholm, this revision—which both clarifies the original text and introduces new and relevant illustrations—became a reality during my initial period as a visiting scholar at the Centre in 2018.

Readers of the 2013 e-book will find the original narrative largely intact, modified where most appropriate, and they will notice substantial new photographs intended to illustrate the book's background principles. New readers will experience a long-form essay, which sets the stage for my later work. I hope that both original and new readers enjoy this re-created volume and consider it an entryway to a rich, sense-based way of thinking about the universals of urbanism that are often set aside without adequate reflection or consideration.

To my chagrin, some have said since the release of the 2013 e-book that "there is no such thing as urbanism without effort." To them, I suggest that the latent forces in the city may play surprisingly prominent roles if we recognize and honor them. It remains critically important to find those urban characteristics that resonate with local culture, and both illustrate and exemplify how change might occur in a more sustainable way.

Stockholm, Sweden
March 7, 2018

Introduction

> What has been is what will be, and what has been done is what will be done; and there is nothing new under the sun.
>
> —*Ecclesiastes 1:9*

CITIES TODAY PRESENT A SENSE OF EXCITEMENT and renewal, and an undeniable focus on more sustainable and inclusive ways of life. A new generation of urban stakeholders boldly experiments with smart city principles, placemaking, and walkable, mixed-use neighborhood settings, including both public space and transit nearby. In the most dedicated urbanist circles, upgraded bicycle and pedestrian infrastructure supplants automobile reliance, "pop-up" places and uses expand, and other creative efforts, such as "parklets," regularly challenge conventional thinking about urban land use and transportation.

Figure 01-A: Vancouver: the livability exemplar.

Figure 01-B: Dublin: transit on display.

Figure 0-2: Madrid: Plaza Mayor: a classical gathering place.

These urban stakeholders—residents, pundits, developers, associated professionals, and politicians—care deeply about city living; they frequently discuss the virtues of urbanism in many ways, including in casual conversation, on social media, or through more applied advocacy. While I find these discussions illuminating and commendable, I often note that even the most ambitious references to transit-oriented development, complete streets, walkability, gentrification versus affordability, or climate change gloss over the basic underpinnings of an authentic urbanism. They underemphasize important cues from the rich backstory of urban history, including unplanned, naturally occurring aspects of city life and foundational examples of non-American venues.

What would we gain from a more deliberate inquiry into the fundamental principles of urban history and organic urban form? Understanding what lies beneath an enticing, well-scaled urban setting—a comfortable sidewalk café, children playing safely in an alleyway—can inform policy and planning efforts that more fully resonate with the particular *culture* and *context* of a place. Without

such a preface of integrity, we are left with merely catchy ideas, plucked from a catalog of trendy, oversubscribed options.

Perhaps ironically, traditional and active close-knit spaces and spontaneous human interactions of the historic city are now key components of a more lively urban future. Contemporary discussions inadvertently embrace familiar approaches that have worked for centuries. In the spirit of both déjà vu and amnesia (concepts combined by American actor/writer Steven Wright[1]), past precedents implicitly live on with once-considered—but often forgotten—core principles ripe for rediscovery.

Why not make today's urbanist efforts even bolder by better explaining their basis and context? I believe we will achieve the most effective evolution of our urban landscapes only if we first challenge ourselves to fully understand the historical underpinnings of the world's most successful cities, towns, and neighborhoods as more than fad or fancy. Successful examples are not always the most well known, but they lie in wait for the interested, discerning observer.

Figure 0-3A: Madrid: safe passage.

Figure 0-3B: Adelaide: green passage.

Figure 0-4: Glasgow: the pedestrian street.

There should be no surprise in this reemergence of familiar elements from historic urban places, nor is it out of style to take notice. Successful community is among the first principles of the human condition, and, at core, city dwellers invariably celebrate environments where they can coexist safely, affordably, and in a mutually supportive way. I believe such celebration is most notable when it occurs spontaneously—seemingly without effort. This effortless experience is the subject of this book. It is what architectural theorist Christopher Alexander called the "natural" versus "artificial" city in his landmark article, "The City Is Not a Tree,"[2] and it occurs more often in organic Old World environments than in new ones. It is premised on the successes of the unpredictable, disjointed, and overlapping, rather than the prescriptive or planned.

As we rethink approaches to urban planning and redevelopment, such organically evolved places—both past and present—offer striking examples of how to reshape the urban environment authentically.[3] Yet contemporary discussions tend to underemphasize the fundamental tension that occurs when the randomly occurring wonders of a naturally changing city are exchanged for programmed approaches to place, such as formulaic development proposals, fashionable land use initiatives, smart city "dashboards," or targeted, theme-based populist campaigns (e.g., various "Pavement to Parks" initiatives[4]).

In fact, whether unintentionally or outright, today's "placemaking" professionals often—with regard to the smallest parklet or the largest plaza—ponder how prescriptive, planned, and programmed efforts can achieve what used to occur naturally and without intervention. Jeff Risom and Myra Madiz described the challenge at length in early 2018, recounting their work in Buenos Aires that focused on the challenges of reconnecting the Villa 31 neighborhood to city services while honoring a preexisting, organic "look and feel" premised on proximity, scale, streets as public spaces, and architectural flexibility.[5]

Figure 0-5: Seattle: from "pavement to park."

I'm also reminded of an essay by Rob Goodspeed that makes a related point.[6] While explaining sociologist Richard Sennett's *The Uses of Disorder*, Goodspeed explains how "smart" visions of city development that indiscriminately mandate technology (light rail) or sustainability-oriented policies (smart growth near transit or work) often miss the real story behind a desired, urbanist "look and feel"—that, in fact, such forms of development were the historical result of authentically evolved complexity, randomness, and conflict over long periods of time. As Daniel Chatman has ironically explained, perhaps the desired ambience of "transit-oriented development" is more important than the transit itself.[7]

Almost 100 years ago, similar discussions surrounded a then-nascent attempt to model "ideal urban neighborhood life." In the

1920s, community planning movement colleagues of Clarence Perry critiqued preliminary formulations of his "neighborhood unit" approach, which was authored as part of the Regional Plan Association's landmark effort to address the repercussions of automobile proliferation, *The Regional Plan of New York and Its Environs*.[8] In 1928, Perry's colleague, the eminent Scottish town planner Thomas Adams, implied the importance of the organic city when he wrote the following:

> Discussions . . . seem to suggest that neighborhood life is something that can be created. All city life is neighborhood life in some form. We should not discuss it as something that is non-existent and can be brought into being, but as something that exists in forms that need to be changed, improved and better organized.[9]

As the discussions continue today, the question of authentic versus prescribed urbanism should remain at the center of urban stakeholder and empowerment dialogues. For example, Trent Noll wrote in *Planetizen*[10] that the naturally occurring basics of placemaking (i.e., comfort, variety, entertainment, and walkability) have existed from time immemorial in successful cities, and today's design challenge is a more purposeful implementation of these basics with a value-engineered mindset to spur investment incentives for savvy developers. I agree with Noll's premise, and, from my perspective, the dialogue should be more visual, more interpretive, and more explicitly focused on the multidisciplinary (and multicultural) underpinnings of urban life.

Understanding the fine-grained history of a place is a gateway to authenticity for today's proffered solutions, and it enhances the quality of local urbanist advocacy and citizen outreach. A healthy dose of urban history is as essential and exciting as it is nostalgic. As I stress throughout this book, it is essential that we spend the time necessary to rediscover, reinterpret, and wisely reapply the long-term calligraphy of interaction between humans and the urban environment. This especially rings true when community—as the essence of this interaction—can be conveyed or supplemented through media that inspire the senses, much like the original experience of "being there."

To those ends, the chapters that follow comprise a visually centered effort examining how we might distinguish underlying, organic relationships between people and cities from indiscriminate prescription—or superficial nostalgia—imposed upon place. I purposefully balance idealism and realism in assessing twenty-first-century urban environments. And I repeatedly underscore the value of individual observation to discern and implement the "urbanism without effort," which I believe is the key to creating lasting and sustainable places.

Chapter 1

The Dynamic Potential of Urbanism Without Effort

As URBAN STAKEHOLDERS—residents, pundits, developers, associated professionals, and politicians—we like to discuss and debate aspects of urbanism[1] and how cities should change to meet new challenges. But when we talk about urbanism, I think we often forget the underlying dynamics that are as old as cities themselves. As a result, we favor fads over the indigenous underpinnings of urban settlement and our own, thorough observations about urban change. We focus too literally on conclusory plans, apps, model codes, transportation modes, building categories, economic and population specifics, and summary indicators of how land is currently used. While we might appropriately champion the programmed successes of certain iconic examples, we risk ignoring the backstory of urban forms and functions and failing to truly understand the traditional relationships between people and place.

I believe it is critical to first isolate spontaneous and latent examples of successful urban land use before applying any data-driven inquiries, prescription of typologies, desired ends, or governmental initiatives. Such inspirational "urbanism without effort" is the premise of this book and its illustrations, as well as the basis for a clean, multidisciplinary slate for reinvigorating the way we think about urban development today.

The Definition

This premise needs a definition and reference point for all that follows here and in future inquiry. Urbanism without effort is what happens naturally when people congregate in cities—based on the innate interactions that urban dwellers have with one another and with the surrounding urban and physical environment. Such innate interactions are often the product of cultural traditions and organic urban development, independent of government intervention, policy, or plan.

Urbanism without effort is not always initially obvious; it may seem more whimsical than remarkable when viewed from an aerial

Figure 1-1: This wall in Paros, Greece, is composed of basic materials left over from previous structures. It shows the fundamental human adaptive spirit at its sustainable best—in local context.

Figure 1-1A: Portions of Seattle's older brick streets remain in certain parts of the city, complemented by more modern pavement types.

photo, an online map, or a satellite picture. In fact, it is almost invisible from these perspectives, as the fine urban grain is lost. It is best recognized and embraced from the ground and experienced firsthand, where it is possible to see more than just the physical outline of the city—it is possible to see life flowing through the urban form.[2] This familiar, firsthand perspective, often informed by photography, focuses on organic and naturally occurring urbanism, as distinguished from other typecast, purposeful approaches, such as tactical, lean, interventionist, insurgent, or "pop-up" urbanism.[3]

While these more purposeful approaches—and associated demonstration projects—may lead to successful places, I often wonder, why don't they always have a meaningful and lasting effect? All too often these approaches are more sensational than not, overly superficial, or temporary by design.[4] And, unless calibrated to the local context, the status quo frequently returns after these purposeful installations, such as street-side tables, greened parking spaces, food trucks, or guerrilla gardens, are removed or abandoned. In comparison, urbanism without effort endures beyond a mere installation or exhibition. Because it is latent rather than faddishly imposed, it can grow and evolve based upon a more historical, authentic, and robust foundation.

Rather than assume that the popular and touted is readily adaptable everywhere, or readily subject to apps, metrics, or labels, we should return to first principles and isolate the fundamental, vernacular relationships between city inhabitants and what surrounds them. We need to look, analyze, and discern, until we remember what a basic and familiar sort of city life looks like. While we consider these inherent factors that shape spaces and their use, we also must remember that there is a certain spontaneous magic attributable to good urban places that can awaken them but will only occur when they are locally relevant and embraced.

The Premise and the Pictures

To assure a successful and meaningful return to first principles, we each need a renewed and fine-tuned qualitative emphasis—our own, image-rich "urban diaries"—over and above the many thoughtful urbanist measures, such as Walk Score,[5] Place Score,[6] StreetScore,[7] or even the conjectural JaneScore.[8] It is time to look at cities in a more holistic way[9] that better explicates today's often irrational fusion of the planned, the spontaneous, and the natural—and to understand the city as "an artefact [*sic*] of a curious kind . . . more like a dream than anything else,"[10] including experiences of place that are "a rainbow well within our grasp."[11]

Urban diaries play an important thematic role in this book and its more applied companion, *Seeing the Better City*,[12] as an ongoing source of urban documentation and understanding. While they may sometimes be figurative, or emerge from an internalized

Figures 1-2 and 1-2A: Human-scale public spaces create a sense of belonging and comfort. The concept is effortless to experience and imagine, as well as a predicate to policy, regulation, and implementation. In a city, stumbling upon—and recording—places like Neal's Yard is undeniably special and can create indelible memories that fit today's dialogue of urbanism. These photos, taken 16 years apart (1997 and 2013), show notable redevelopment, but this small courtyard in London's Covent Garden section retains a time-honored focus on holistic-health restaurants, shops, and businesses—accessible through a narrow passage off of Monmouth Street—a reminder of why walking-oriented guides or articles are often the best "radar" to use for touring a city.

memory or intuition, they may also take the form of a notebook, a scrapbook, a sketchbook, or a digital file displayed by computer or tablet that reflects changing views of the city over time.

No matter what form an urban diary may take, I believe (and *Seeing the Better City* explains and applies) that well-composed, onsite photographs are an essential part of documenting holistic urban observation, beyond the removed convenience of Google Street View. Whether immediately tangible or a picture in the mind, such imagery can re-create what political writer Alexander Cockburn once termed "the lost valleys of the imagination."[13]

Legendary travel photographer Burton Holmes aptly used the phrase "film as biography" to describe photographs that authentically capture another time or another place.[14] To me, that term infers principles of practice for regulation and design that are easily observed from images of real and foundational places. In particular, the architect is able to derive the relation between building and street. The traffic engineer finds inspiration for lanes, surfacing, and signage. The lawyer and planner see building setbacks and the means to encourage pedestrian spaces while assuring light, air, acceptable noise levels, and governance of private use of public spaces.

No doubt, I inherited this point of view from my father, who was an urban planning professor. While growing up, I watched him photograph, with an East German Exacta, for purposes of his later sketching, teaching, and advocating the role of urban imagery. In a 1965 article, he argued that several landmark studies of American communities (e.g., Lloyd Warner's *Yankee City*[15] and Robert and Helen Lynd's *Middletown*[16]) partially missed the mark because they lacked diagrams and pictures.

> Many social studies of communities refer implicitly or explicitly to urban form without so much as a picture, map or diagram. Yet visual material can make a contribution to understanding the urban environment itself, the interrelationship of society and environment, and the development of techniques for study and communication.[17]

Figures 1-3 and 1-3A: Urban diarists collecting information in Lisbon and Marseilles.

Figure 1-4: Rovinj, Croatia, by author at age 13; honoring the water.

Figure 1-5: Udine, Italy, by author at age 13; important public place.

My own 1968 photographs from Slovenia, Croatia, and Italy (partially shown here) document my first interests in reading the city for myself, something we can easily do on a much larger, more shareable scale today with smartphones and social media platforms such as Instagram and Facebook. Even without digital outlets, as a teenage beneficiary of my father's academic research, I was drawn to the differences I saw in foreign cities that predate my native Seattle by more than 1,000 years, specifically the following:

- Cities that organized around important public places, like churches and squares and towers
- Monuments located in these public places, some new and some that have been there a very long time, to honor people or events from history
- Notable walking areas where people were separated from cars
- Cities that honored the water around them, and built themselves so that land uses were clustered close together and work was close to home
- Cities where, in the face of a wall, there were different, exposed layers from several eras, that told the story of how the city grew

In the past 20 years, I've restarted this search for expressions of effortless urbanism in other places in order to compare and contrast the American experience. Journeys to common and uncommon destinations—ranging from Australia to the Middle East to Tanzania to Malta and Iceland—have illuminated the primary patterns of human settlement and land use, with a focus on enviable practices derived from the historical lessons of climate, culture, and the core needs of human life. This dance of people and place can be painfully simple when experienced and photographed in context, with fundamental tenets in mind and history displayed outright. The roles of walking, shelter, and movement between places, and the impacts of climate and safety appear far more basic and robust through the lens of careful observation from across the world.

In 2009, I began building on vignettes observed both through this international lens as well as through local examples, and since then I have depicted and described a range of urban basics in several articles, in the first edition of this book, and in its 2017 companion, *Seeing the Better City*.[18] These efforts and associated social media frame, inter alia, huts and fortresses, carts and bicycles, and narrow paths and boulevards—and include narrative and photographs that feature places, spaces, buildings, and people as they appear in context, often by happenstance. As a result, I rediscovered perspectives that led me to address local issues—even in law practice—more focused on the implicit and organic evolution of urbanized areas rather than immediately embracing incomplete, nostalgic, popularized and/or prescribed urbanist and "smart city" labels, metrics, or points of view.

Polarities and Outliers

Sometimes, in my opinion, we overemphasize the virtues of the city—or latch on to the next popular urbanist notion or trend—without adequate precedential or contextual inquiry.

In the extreme, to paraphrase Lennon and McCartney, we can easily "misunderstand all that we see" amid a placemaking approach once bluntly critiqued by the late Ada Louise Huxtable, "[t]he remarkable marriage of technologically based and shrewdly programmed artificial experience with a manufactured and managed environment."[19] Huxtable made a discerning point, that somehow in envisioning the city, reality was not the only option, and the glorified fake risked carrying the day. As she noted in 1997:

> The dream of pedestrianism, so valiantly and fruitlessly pursued by planners who have looked to the past and overseas for models of historic hill towns and plazas . . . has been aggressively naturalized; the social stroll has become a sensuous assault.[20]

Figure 1-6: In Las Vegas, the inspiration of a French town square sets the stage for slot machines rather than public assembly.

Figure 1-7: Las Vegas: the Paris, context askew.

Figure 1-8: Las Vegas: the Venetian, replete with automobile.

Figure 1-8A: Stockholm, Gamla stan: historic old town, or touristic shell?

In the intervening years, have we grown toward greater authenticity? For example, Eugene, Oregon's pedestrian mall didn't always work as planned.[21] However, Arlington, Virginia's pervasive focus on sustainability and alternative modes of transportation has broadened awareness and approach, and created the countervailing successes of transit-oriented development.[22] As, generally, has Portland, Oregon's modern legacy of light rail, streetcars, and bicycles. Whatever the answer to the question of authenticity, we should consider the risks of places with a purpose to provide only an illusion—nothing more—of places where we may want to be. Such places end up as little more than a hollow reminder of their authentic inspiration. To quote Shakespeare's King Lear, "nothing will come of nothing."[23]

According to journalist-turned-urban authority Grady Clay, there is more work to be done than casual emulation of inspirational examples. The "undisclosed evidence" underlying the authentic form and patterns of cities is invaluable, yet often goes undiscovered. In *Close-Up: How to Read the American City*, Clay wrote:

> And where are we? Grasping at straws, clutching yesterday's program, swamped by today's expert view, clawing at the newest opinion polls, but neglecting that limitless, timeless, boundless wealth of visible evidence that merely waits in a potentially organizable state for us to take a hard look, to make the next move.[24]

As I explain in *Seeing the Better City*, in the years since Huxtable's and Clay's writing, the merit of a city-dweller's individual, personal observation and exploration may have lost further ground to popular, competing camps of typologies and endless debate about which should prevail.

The more prescriptive, neotraditional attributes of first-generation new urbanism and form-based codes arguably flirted with Huxtable's warning against Disney-fied developments (including the well-known new urbanist-inspired model town in Celebration,

Florida,[25] which was in fact built by Disney). In addition to the more spontaneous, interventionist approaches, such as tactical, insurgent, or "pop-up" urbanism noted earlier (increasingly embraced by many new urbanists today[26]), other more recent trends include landscape urbanism,[27] "green" or low-impact development,[28] bicycle infrastructure, and a considerable focus on compact and walkable transit-oriented development. All of these approaches share an implicit, if not explicit goal—*behavior modification* through planning and design—in order to build community and teach sustainable ways of urban life.

Consider how a purpose-driven acknowledgment or inventory—an urban diary—of urbanism without effort might precede these "pied piper" interventions. Ideas should not be vetted and advanced without an eye to the indigenous urban spirit, with its ready and simple victories ripe for observation, in parts of the city less known or described. Simply stated, spontaneous, organic neighborhood life can be readily illustrated by each of us and is already there for the taking.

Figure 1-9: From the organic in Seattle . . .

Figure 1-10: . . . to the programmed in Melbourne, Carlton, with similar results.

On the one hand, naturally occurring phenomena such as an "alley movie night" (further described in chapter 3) laudably evolve without policy or design. At first, this small-scale urbanism may seem unremarkable, but its success is assured through simple, spontaneous actions of neighbors—an important reminder that a city neighborhood can experience community without really trying—an urbanism without effort that needs no thought leadership or sound bites.

The organic synergy of "alley movie night" among neighbors replicates the latent familiarity of European street life, not because of doctrine or dogma, but because, as depicted above, it is as natural as affiliation with the place next door. By comparison, more purposeful and programmed approaches,[29] such as Melbourne's Moonlight Cinema on the Botanic Gardens lawn, or Cinema Nights in Melbourne's Piazza Italia (in the predominantly Italian district of Carlton) feature passersby joining neighbors for an organized event—more an imitation of an ideal than bona fide urbanism without effort. But it creates, nonetheless, a delightful dissonance by placing a neighborhood-like activity within the larger-scale confines of a busy city.

In contrast, while the organic can provide a sound basis for emulation, policy, and implementation, disparate prescriptions of urban form can have the opposite effect, even beyond Huxtable's admonitions. Sometimes, the look and feel of a place may seem inspirational as an urban scale worth repeating. But, in fact, the underlying reasons for its appearance may be the polar opposite from the ideal, sustainable city model.

To me, one such example has particular irony: the Ghetto in the Cannareggio section of Venice appears to be a compact, dense urban development of the sort touted by today's urbanists. However, further investigation reveals a sordid history of overcrowding and segregation.

While the Venetian Ghetto[30] has the same dense, walkable core that is so desirable today, in the sixteenth century it was built to house a disfavored religious and cultural group that was allowed to work in the remainder of the city only by day. The Ghetto was an isolated island where the bridges were locked at night, effectively imprisoning the residents. The institutionalization of the term "ghetto" helps to reveal the backstory of the buildings, structures, and spaces, and that the full sociocultural story of a place should be vetted before its form is borrowed elsewhere.

Figure 1-11: Venice, Ghetto: at first glance, a tasteful and compact new urbanist venue?

These polarities of organic success in an American neighborhood alley versus formalistic dysfunction of the Venetian Ghetto illustrate the diversity and depth of urban experience. Looks can deceive, and context and history play a large role in the level of success of an urban place. However, without a careful, contextual archaeology of the urban landscape, onlookers may not readily understand the social and/or physical backdrop at hand.

Similarly, what of larger-scale outliers—affecting entire towns or regions—where the look and feel of the built environment are uniquely affected by socioeconomic forces, only discernible through bona fide investigation?

The form of urban settlements and appearance of constituent structures reflect underlying culture and regulation, and in times of change, buildings, landscapes, and objects transform to show the impact of new or modified policies or rules. As Emily Talen has so capably summarized in *City Rules*,[31] the resulting shapes of compliance—such as the patterns of height, bulk, and density dictated by a new downtown zoning code—can potentially reinvent the urban landscape. But "shapes of avoidance" can also dramatically alter the urban landscape.

Consider, in the context of everyday urbanism, those shapes and patterns dictated by focused avoidance of regulation. Here, I am not discussing just spontaneous parklets, impromptu bike lanes, and sidewalk tables of "guerrilla urbanism" or "pop-up" cities, but widespread examples of urban forms that result when policy or regulation is creatively defied. Call it the urban landscape's manifestation of French-American microbiologist René Dubos's classic discourses on remarkable and unpredictable human adaptation to environmental change, *Man Adapting*[32] and *So Human an Animal*.[33]

A compelling example is the alteration of a southern Italian landscape in the fifteenth to seventeenth centuries premised on the avoidance of taxes or fees—the apparent explanation for the unique shape of *trulli* houses in Puglia, Italy—and the resulting appearance of the Itria Valley and the town of Alberobello.[34]

As the story goes, local inhabitants built the conical houses—that don't look like houses—without mortar. This method allowed easy destruction, so the Counts of Conversano could avoid property tax payments to the King of Naples on permanent structures (such as residences).

In summary, a one-size-fits-all typology or summary number is unlikely to facilitate desired outcomes. An overemphasis on physical form or a particular policy, without an eye to underlying cultural and socioeconomic factors, may create unintended consequences. Urbanism without effort depends on initial acknowledgment of local values and preferences as a central aspect of creating successful urban environments.

Figure 1-12: Alberobello: the trulli, *"shape of avoidance."*

Figure 1-13: Alberobello: historical view.

Rediscovering the Effortless Urbanist Fabric

When we are able to recognize and communicate the kind of holistic context that leads to urbanism without effort, only then can we understand the most appropriate solutions for the modern stage. Notably, this is not a new assertion—some would say it's Jane Jacobs's legacy, echoed by Roberta Brandes Gratz almost 30 years ago, with her praise in *The Living City* for preservation of historic neighborhoods and prosecution of "expert" redevelopment plans.[35]

But my focus both here and in *Seeing the Better City* goes further, and is more than a nostalgia-based framework, or preservation for preservation's sake. It is a call for critically understanding places—ideally based on personal experience, familiarity, and observation, before prescribing solutions—and the discriminating application of approaches that *work in context*. It is one that needs amplification in today's dialogue, which, based on assumed goals of equity, empowerment, sustainability, and livable places, often advances urbanist or sustainability agendas indiscriminately, whether through the Internet or social media or via provocative advocacy of smart cities, placemaking, density, affordability, or a return to healthier and more efficient transportation modes.

Between the polarities of success and dysfunction, as I've already outlined, and careful observation of today's cities and towns, as championed by Clay and others, we can discern and reclaim the basic relationships between humans and urban environments leading us to lay the basis for a new effortless urban fabric.

Architectural historian and critic Joseph Rykwert emphasized the personal nature and importance of the underlying, multidisciplinary urban dynamic. And twentieth-century writers Lewis Mumford and J. B. Jackson often described these human–urban relationships as buried—even lost—but rediscoverable through a core understanding of urban history that is more humanistic than quantifiable.

Underlying Factors

From Melbourne to Barcelona to Buenos Aires, an existing fabric of large, vehicular-oriented avenues and squares simultaneously thrives with pedestrian life. Wide sidewalks, engaged storefronts, seating areas, second-floor verandas, and careful lighting and use of color work cohesively with lanes of travel, creating popular, well-frequented thoroughfares.

What are the underlying factors that create such hybrid examples of vital city life? How might they apply to cities in search of renewed vitality? Whether the answer is premised on climate, cultural patterns, urban density, tourism, or a combination, the point is to first derive contextual clues by a personal investigation of, and return to, the more effortless city we have lost.

Figure 1-14: Barcelona: Passeig de Sant Joan, multimodal view.

Rykwert, in *The Seduction of Place*, describes this urban evolution as a constant interaction of planned and unplanned efforts of citizens, officials, and institutions combining to morph the city over time.[36] I believe that Rykwert's focus remains highly relevant, as globalization furthers the unplanned contrasts of vernacular building forms and more uniform, commercially driven building features. In one example that I recently observed, a portion of the landmark Lisbon train station was adapted to house a Starbucks location, consistent with a corporate adaptive reuse policy that began with the company's Seattle headquarters. In a broader setting, in 2011, the Urban Land Institute's initial "What's Next? Real Estate in the New Economy" report[37] explained how faster-paced workdays, telecommuting, and other changes to the work environment are driving multiple modifications to the appearance, form, and function of urban space.

Figure 1-15: Stockholm: the new Odenplan, with people and transit hub in mind.

Has the determination of city image and form become the purview of a chosen few, or can the return of citizens to firsthand observation (and the experience of neighborhood or city-making) enhance the urbanism without effort discussed here and in *Seeing the Better City*? According to Rykwert:

> The success of a city . . . cannot be measured in terms of financial growth and of a share in those markets it may have managed to capture, or even of its place in the process of globalization which is the inescapable phenomenon of our time—but depends on the inherent strength of the fabric and its availability to the social forces that mold the life of its inhabitants.[38]

The Precedent

Mumford's epic 1961 inquiry into urban origins and prospects, *The City in History*,[39] addresses important, first principles of urbanization and their fundamental relationship to modern land use, transportation, and the evolution of technology. He describes how urban origins embraced the basic human social disposition to commune in the context of the hunter-gatherer framework. He then evokes an evolution from caves to crossroads, premised on the two poles of human life: "movement and settlement," a relationship at the heart of how cities work.

Through these fundamentals, Mumford also explained the gradual change from the city as premised on human needs to gather, settle, and move to a perception and organization of the city based on a plan view. Examples include the monumental planning ideals of the nineteenth century, such as long, straight, wide streets prime for military function (with accompanying landmarks at the ends) and the development of imposing impressive vistas, characteristic of L'Enfant's plan for Washington, D.C., and Haussmann's renovation of Paris. The outcome was to mask the human scale and to create barriers to pedestrian movement in favor of wide avenues, which became, unwittingly, readily adaptable to the automobile.[40]

Figure 1-16: Edinburgh: a laboratory of learning about the rich interplay of Scotland and England, and how the time before unification shaped urban form.

Similarly, Jackson's "The Discovery of the Street"[41] examines the wondrous and ethereal about life in cities. Through a bittersweet history of public space, from medieval markets to the modern freeway, he weaves an ambiguous tale about what has become the raison d'être of today's urbanism—reclaiming the human and natural systems that underlie the city, as urban reemergence from within, rather than sprawl to afar. Jackson invoked a laudable challenge to the post-freeway world—a challenge reliant on urbanism without effort—to remember the importance of the first person-based, organic landscape of neighborhoods, towers, and spires lost before we can remember.[42]

The main point for invoking Rykwert, Mumford, and Jackson today is that in order to achieve a successful city with minimal effort—a place of congregation in the social science, rather than

Figure 1-16A: Richmond upon Thames, England: reclaiming the first-person landscape.

the religious, sense—we must understand the backstory of organic human association, settlement, and transportation. We must further honor the implicit inquiry of such authors as to *why* stones and huts—density based on human association and interdependence—evolved into modern-day public and private spaces with the associated loss of a human scale.

Enhancing the Urban Fabric: Acknowledgment and Approach

Today, acknowledgment of this fundamental urban fabric often lacks either the lost art of illustrative storytelling of the Mumford–Jackson tradition or Rykwert's style of emphasis on the blended forces that underlie city life. While contemporary authorities, such as Copenhagen-based Jan Gehl and related Gehl Institute work, reference universal human affinities for public space and list key features and methods to activate spaces across cultures,[43] the resulting prescriptions for change risk interpretation as overly generic, or conclusory.

In addition to the range of purposeful approaches that I referenced earlier, such as tactical, insurgent, or pop-up urbanism, over the last 25 years we have seen the tension increase between two camps within the architecture and design world—that of Rem Koolhaas and his monumental, building-based urbanism, and its polar opposite, first-generation new urbanism's neotraditional re-creation of a small-town, pre-automobile look and feel. Koolhaas's civic focus on the central place of a building declared "urbanism is dead."[44] Where is the middle ground?

Within the last 10 years, in reinventing cities like Detroit, new urbanists such as Andres Duany shifted attention to "lean urbanism," focused on regulatory streamlining and away from one-size-fits-all zoning administration. Another proffered middle-ground solution is John Kaliski's "everyday urbanism," which celebrates the ordinary, the banal, and the mundane, partially in response to the sanitized versions of urbanism presented over the past century. In his *Everyday Urbanism* essay "The Present City and the Practice of City Design," Kaliski notes: "architects and urban designers are typically taught to design toward stasis. Any notion of urban stability, however, is sooner or later contradicted by the city's inherent flux."[45]

While these varied approaches include celebration of the mundane as much as the extraordinary features of the urban environment, I believe that urbanism without effort goes a critical step further, by *first* examining the fundamental origin and appeal of particular urban settings, and *only then* determining how the answers contextually apply the process of invigorating place.

The idea of urbanism without effort is a result of understanding not only what makes good space but also the constant evolution of the underlying social, political, and economic contexts of the

Figure 1-17: Paris: celebration of the mundane.

Figure 1-18: Portland: more of the everyday.

city. As Rykwert would likely opine, such collective behavior continues to shape the way we use space and interact with our fellow residents.

Learning from Urbanism Without Effort

What are lessons learned and best practices that emerge from studying urbanism without effort, and how do these differ from the aforementioned, more purposeful monikers and short-term approaches? How can we take such lessons and practices, use them to guide our planning efforts, and apply them meaningfully to our urban environments? Physical form, replicated without thought to local socioeconomic conditions, may appear to have the characteristics of successful urban places but in reality can lead to drastically different results.

In answer to these questions, the remainder of this book applies the principles set forth in both the introduction and this chapter. Chapter 2 provides an overview of fundamental interactions of humans and the urban environment—and how they can be observed and manifested as urbanism without effort. Chapter 3 presents specific case studies and illustrated vignettes, selected from my collection of photographs and observations, touching on themes, elements, and examples of urbanism without effort from across the world.

In conclusion, chapter 4 reexamines this book's premise, with a practical gloss. Urbanism without effort is important for people to understand as a baseline for today's urban adaptation, innovation, and creation of more livable places. The chapter presents a five-part inquiry in developing urban planning initiatives and the associated regulatory policy and subsequent implementation, much of which I develop to a greater extent in *Seeing the Better City*. In general, the inquiry proceeds from diary, to contextual understanding, to an adaptability analysis under local conditions, followed by a more practical inquiry of available policy avenues and implementation possibilities.

I believe the best urbanism is often the urbanism we already have, and that understanding the organic nature of this urbanism without effort is key. Accordingly, taken together, the remaining chapters suggest how we can strategically create opportunities for our cities to evolve sustainably, while providing room for the dynamic, unexpected elements of human settlement and movement that are the urban legacy.

Chapter 2

Observing Urbanism Without Effort at Work—The Human Experience

URBANISM WITHOUT EFFORT honors the crossroads of human nature and urban life. It is at the heart of why neighbors often collaborate without hesitation, public markets and street fairs regain popularity, street dining occurs outside of restaurants, and old buildings seamlessly evolve to new uses. It illustrates circumstances where people feel safe and explains underlying reasons for the appearance and configuration of buildings, adjoining streets, and spaces that connect and surround them. It cuts beneath technology, or the practical issues of politics, policy, and process, and focuses on the inadvertent elements of place and interconnection.

If urbanism without effort is built on fundamental relationships between humans and the urban environment, it makes sense to further isolate those relationships, to analyze what they are and what they look like, since understanding these innate relationships can explain their desirability and roles in the evolution of our cities.

Figure 2-1: Porto: passing by.

Figure 2-1A: Calenzana: innate relationships of people and place.

Figure 2-1B: Paris, Luxembourg Gardens: fundamental relationships that span a lifetime.

What is the human experience of place that is inherently a part of city life?[1] According to Rykwert, the answer has changed from the dictated certainty of ancient times to *each individual's experience* with the surrounding city.

> The Roman who walked along the *cardo* knew that his walk was the axis around which the sun turned, and that if he followed the *decamanus*, he was following the sun's course. The whole universe and its meaning were spelled out in his civic institutions—so he was at home in it. We have lost all of the beautiful certainty of the way the world works . . . this does not absolve us from looking for some ground of certainty in our attempts to give form to the human environment. *It is no longer likely that we shall find this ground in the world which the cosmologists are continually reshaping around us and so we must look for it inside ourselves: in the constitution and structure of the human person* [emphasis added].[2]

Harvard professor John Stilgoe also argues for the role of each individual and his or her personal observation of the built environment. The title of Stilgoe's most noted book, *Outside Lies Magic*,[3] sets the tone for self-inquiry. Grady Clay agrees, and heightens the importance of individual interpretation of the city.

> Experts may help assemble data, specialists may organize it, professionals may offer theories to explain it. But none of these can substitute for each person's own leap into the dark, jumping in to draw his or her own conclusions.[4]

Tony Hiss, in *The Experience of Place*, also pays particular attention to the innate sense-based, "simultaneous perception" of city-dwellers—often in response to commonly overlooked elements of the urban environment (e.g., his oft-cited passage about the Grand Central Terminal concourse in New York City).[5]

In my experience, a helpful way to catalog elements of each person's relationship to his or her city is in the form of an "urban diary." An urban diary can account for the context of history, culture, and

Figure 2-2: Stresa, Lago Di Maggiore: sensing place.

Figure 2-3: Matera: finding meaning in place.

climate of a particular urban place, and recognize instances of urbanism without effort at work. My urban diary has always been photocentric, and I have followed this approach in my articles and in the vignettes contained in chapter 3. As noted earlier, *Seeing the Better City* embraces the urban diary fundamentals explored here, and carries them forward to direct application by citizens, design professionals, real estate developers, municipal staff, and elected officials.

The Baseline Urban Diary—A Tool of Personal Observation

Understanding Place

A prevalent theme in contemporary urbanist articles, blog posts,[6] and social media feeds[7] addresses the enhanced experience of places in cities—whether while walking, biking, or using public transportation. An exemplary article is Kasey Klimes's reflective personal essay on bicycles as keys to better cities,[8] as it centers on and celebrates this very key point of "experiential understanding" of place. The premise is simple: cities are hubs of human interaction, and the urban experience can be enhanced by authentic participation in the dynamics of a place and transitions to nearby venues, including other neighborhoods or, in certain instances, nearby towns.

For instance, in the quest to define human relationships with the surrounding city, it is helpful to consider typical, everyday journeys within an urban environment.[9] We usually begin every trip on foot, starting from a private place, such as a house or apartment. In order to reach the next place, we often use at least one other mode of transit. Meanwhile, others simultaneously travel in similar ways. Our paths cross, and transit modes further diversify. If we stop and look around, we see a system of mutually crossed paths that define the urban experience. The public realm exists amid and between these paths—streets, sidewalks, squares, and parks that are subject to regulation addressing appropriate conduct, health, safety, and land use.

Figure 2-4: Seattle: a diary walk in the Madrona neighborhood.

Figures 2-4A and 2-4B: Antibes: the journeys home.

The places we experience in this innate urban fabric hold the embedded patterns that we should uncover, read, and reinterpret. Documenting this "evidence" is one aspect of creating the urban diary[10] (now well documented in *Seeing the Better City*) and is consistent with the "experiential understanding" outlined so far:

> [R]ather than merely watching someone else's video, might you further develop and understand your relationship to place, as well as other similar interactions which you observe?[11]

Creating an urban diary is a kind of archaeology that involves more than unearthing distinct artifacts from another era. While urban diaries can be figurative or memory based, we can also tangibly record our explorations with whatever tool we choose, such as a pen for writing or sketching, a keyboard for typing, or a camera for capturing images. Each tool requires active interaction with a place by recording and making note of its underlying relationships. For me, it includes observing the place-based impacts of four interactive factors, building on the classic settlement-movement continuum:

1. The intersection of the built and natural environments
2. The evolution of transportation modes
3. The application of associated land use plans and regulations
4. The continuation and/or evolution of surrounding land uses

One of the most compelling aspects of an urban diary is finding vantage points in the city where people easily watch people—essentially small-scale human observatories. From such places, we sit on the edges of the public realm and create so-called urban mirrors. Using these mirrors, we look in at human conduct much like our own, to be reminded of who we really are. Such places are often indicative of safe public environments, including active streets, corners, and squares. They are particularly prevalent in

Figure 2-5: Paris: looking up in the city.

Figure 2-5A: Matera: looking in the urban mirror.

cultures where neighbors readily interact, and the seams between public and private are softer than zoning setbacks, while still allowing for a private world.

Personal documentation and contemplation of the journey from place to space—crossing and intersecting and embracing edges of the public and private realms—may be the best way to understand where we live, the choices we make, and those that are made for us. Through such urban diaries—whether written, captured in photos, or merely careful mental observations—each of us can learn more about cities as they are or could be.

The cities we seek should include these small places where, when the bustle of life begins in the morning and evening, people interact with facets of the city around them. I suspect that workable density in the city of the future will abound with these types of spaces readily ascertainable from cities of the past.

Examining Innate People–Place Relationships

The opportunity to draw back and observe the actions of "getting there, going there, and almost there," and then "being there," yields memorable snapshots of daily urban life. Such snapshots of the interaction of people and places illustrate far more than our best spectator sport: as urban mirrors, they visually describe salient points of public–private interface, frame the quality of the urban experience, and—most importantly—define the following innate, urbanism without effort relationships of city-dwellers to their urban surroundings:

- An organic *mixture* of built and natural environments and workable allocations of public and private space which interact in a way that creates vitality rather than segregation
- A *marriage* of movement and settlement (land use and transportation) with components worthy of replication because origin, destination, and travel between is interesting, safe, and relatively efficient

Figure 2-6: France, Portugal, United States: who we really are.

- A *combination* of circumstances accomplishing adaptive re-use of the preexisting built environment, consistent with sustainability principles
- A *blending* of traditional urban conduct—to walk, to use wheeled vehicles sensibly and safely with mixed modes side by side, to share resources, to have visual variety and a range of uses for a place
- An *interplay* of factors leading to comfortable community and neighborhood, and related collaboration and safety without significant government intervention.

The Innate People–Place Relationships: Illustrated

Sustainability as the Organic Mixture of Built and Natural Environments

The building blocks of the sustainable city combine to produce innate, effortless relationships between humans and the city that are worthy of attention. The word "sustainability" has been used and repurposed in many contexts, but in the built environment, "sustainability" refers to the economic, environmental, and social dimensions, all of which work together to create what is commonly called the "triple bottom line." The seminal definition of sustainable development can be found in the United Nations Brundtland Report (*Our Common Future*) of 1987.[12]

> Sustainable development is development that meets the needs of the present without compromising the ability of future generations to meet their own needs.[13]

Parallels emerge between instances of urbanism without effort, sustainable development, adaptive reuse, and historic preservation.

According to former Barcelona councilmember and Harvard professor Joan Busquets, the most sustainable cities integrate natural geography and systems (such as water) into the urban fabric, provide a comfortable city center, and have long-lasting, flexible designs. His formula for a merger of geography, comfort, and flexibility embraces many issues in today's urban dialogue, such as increasing opportunities to walk and use transit, to live closer to work, and to consequently increase density and the efficient use of urban space.[14]

Busquets also described the sustainable city as the historical city, which to me suggests a physical realm of the sort championed by Mumford and Jackson, and the late Edmund Bacon. In Bacon's 1967 classic, *Design of Cities*,[15] he looks to understand cities based on the historical and traditional patterned interplay between people and place. Like this book and *Seeing the Better City*, Bacon considers this interplay as a rich underpinning for modern planning, regulatory, and design approaches.

Using Busquets's hypothesis as a foundation, a sustainable city also tactfully manages the transition from rural to urban, from country to city. Today's tools seek to enhance this symbiotic town and country relationship through metropolitan regional planning efforts and often more innovative approaches lobbied by nongovernmental organizations, such as Forterra (formerly the Cascade Land Conservancy) in the Pacific Northwest. Forterra has pioneered incentives for rural conservation in return for more concentrated urban development in urbanized portions of Washington State.[16]

How did this physical transition from country to city occur in the past? How was the change in surroundings designed—or not—as one approached the city center? In the quotation at the beginning of the chapter, Rykwert reminds us that over time, the uniformity of baseline Roman plans aligned to the sun's behavior and yielded to less structured, personal interpretations of the surrounding city. I think we have something to learn by reclaiming from our collective memory the important, embedded pattern of city streets and alleys. We should acknowledge this pattern not just as transportation conduits but as anticipation-enhancing guides for travelers' arrival at

Figures 2-7 and 2-7A: Dublin and London: attributes of a comfortable city center.

Figure 2-8: Uppsala: the flexible city on the road to the square.

focal points of commerce, government, and public squares. What was the foundational role of angles and curves, color and light, all modified by architectural features, elevations, and building materials?

Today's urban developers often prioritize aggregation of smaller land parcels, and land assembly and complete or partial demolition often constitute the first phases of redevelopment. This approach does not always mesh well with Busquets's more abstract formulation of geography, comfort, and flexibility. But his formulation is an important reference point for how inhabitants have best blended with urban environments in the past, as a precedent for prioritizing a more organic urbanism without effort today.

Marriage of Movement and Settlement

Embedded in Busquets's sustainable city is the familiar duality of movement and settlement championed by Mumford, as discussed in chapter 1. The most fundamental innate relationship of humans and cities marries the adventure of movement with the security of settlement. To Mumford, cities grew with technologies that expanded the capacity to move and made greater travel distances more achievable. Today's focus on the relationships between land use and transportation is centered on this relationship, as is the modern quest to locate inhabitants closer to workplaces so that daily access routes are walkable or served by public transit.

An ideal city, for Mumford, echoes Busquets's, and blends and balances nature and technology. It is also a multidisciplinary, dynamic entity where the innate elements of movement and settlement combine in support of vital aspects of urban life as summarized by Mumford.

> The essential physical means of a city's existence are the fixed site, the durable shelter, the permanent facilities for assembly, interchange, and storage. . . . The city in its complete sense, then, is a geographic plexus, an economic organization, an institutional process, a theater of social action, and an aesthetic symbol of collective unity. The city fosters art and is art; the city creates the theater and is the theater. It is in the city, the city as theater, that man's more purposive activities are focused, and work out, through conflicting and co-operating personalities, events, groups into more significant culminations.[17]

Circumstances Adopting Adaptive Reuse

Many of the examples in this book describe places or buildings that have undergone adaptive reuse—co-opting existing buildings for a new purpose. As depicted in the photograph of the eclectic wall in Paros, Greece, in chapter 1, adaptive reuse is part of human nature as a response to limited resources and a time-honored element of effortless urbanism. To the observer, adaptive reuse can provide a legible stratigraphy of a place.

As our surroundings evolve, we can create incentives and inspiration for transformational places that are sustainable in form and function and pay attention to the past. An example in chapter 3 profiles the long-term evolution of the urban core of Split, Croatia,

Figures 2-9, 2-9A, and 2-9B: Nice: multimodal blending of tram and pedestrian in Place Massena.

Figure 2-10: Nice: blending biking and waterfront assets on Promenade d'Anglais.

where, by practical necessity, the remains of the retirement palace of the Roman emperor Diocletian evolved and became the center of a modern city.

In "The Necessity for Ruins,"[18] Jackson noted, "Ruins provide the incentive for restoration, and for a return to origins." He called for the proactive use of ruins to reclaim what worked before: throughout history, cities have provided venues for cultural, economic, and religious transactions as both centers of settlement and qualitative measures of human habitat. To reinvent them (or juxtapose the best of the past with the present or future), we need to dissect feelings of nostalgia and more affirmatively understand where we have been and where we are going, at more than the scale of individual buildings.

The increasingly popular placemaking movement is ideally suited to offset any sense that we have let "local place" wither away—as reinvigorating publicly accessible spaces provides the opportunity to rediscover what Jackson termed a past golden age—"a time when we seek to restore the world around us to something like its former beauty." Opportunities for more citizen involvement emerge from many types of places, functional and symbolic. Shown here, the vital Easter community of St. Peter's Square in Rome, and a stream of visitors to the ancient amphitheater in Arles, France, give way to the evolved, rustic, sea-oriented town of Port Townsend, Washington.

Here we see transformative places. While function of buildings can evolve, the vitality of place remains as our senses witness new

Figures 2-11 and 2-11A: Vatican City: continual vitality of place in St. Peter's Square and Arles: Amphitheater.

Figure 2-12: Port Townsend: form retained.

contexts for human interaction with tradition, time, and transport. Perhaps now more touristic than pious, the realm of gladiators, or seafaring, such places live on.

Collections of remaining buildings are only one part of a surviving organic urban pattern. Vestiges of former transit modes can be repurposed as well. For example, in Seattle's Leschi neighborhood, the city of 2018 overlays the city of 1930. As the use of automobiles increased, infrastructure, such as a former cable car bridge, became obsolete. In 1940, the cable car line was abandoned and replaced by a bus line.

Images of Frink Park (a portion of Seattle's 1903 Olmsted park plan) are consistent with today's urbanist ideals, and show the

Figure 2-13: Seattle: Frink Park— the old transit fabric meets the new

juxtaposition of the bridge, bicyclist, and pedestrian working together to create a locus. On the old track bed, a piece of the park now continues and becomes a trail through the hillside woods above and nearby. Moving forward, we should design and regulate in a way that the inadvertence described here becomes more purposeful, enabling sustainable reuse on a broader scale.

Latent Urban Conduct Observed in Place

Common, latent characteristics of urban communities contribute to the heterogeneity of interesting, adaptable, desirable places. However, not all characteristics are present in all places at all times—the combination of factors is particular to each place, and what works well for one culture and place is not necessarily right for another.

What are the common characteristics, and how do they interact? How do the pieces work together to create more than just an assemblage?

- Density and street life illustrate the marriage of movement and settlement and activate corners, squares, and streets around the clock, with pedestrian-scale buildings and street furniture.
- Mixed modes of transit—pedestrian, bicycle, car, public transportation—interact in a way that facilitates safety without strict separation. Pedestrians can navigate and explore easily with signage and paths.
- Spaces are available to stay, sit, stand, and watch other people. Similarly, places are readily apparent for other human basics—to eat and drink, and to obtain shelter from the sun, wind, rain, and snow.
- Porous boundaries—fences with gates, changes in pavement and elevations, stairs, doors, windows—demarcate what is private, semiprivate, and public, and allow for movement and views in or out.
- Landmarks, visually interesting architecture, flora and fauna, color, and water also facilitate participation in the urban environment by all ages.

Figures 2-14 and 2-14A: Otranto and Melbourne: latent human conduct.

Figures 2-15 and 2-15A: Nice and Aveiro: children and space, safely.

If this compendium of urbanism has been achieved without effort, it is usually the result of organic evolution over the course of many years. New projects or larger developments that are built at one identifiable date risk sacrificing the often "gritty" visual complexity and richness that result from long-term assembly through the accretion of time.

For example, in Italy's Puglia region, the dynamism of place is intrinsic to climate and tradition and more naturally occurs amid commerce and curiosity, along streets, beside buildings, and as a component of cross-town strolls. This dynamism can be read in faces, the simplicity of child's play, and nearby mealtime banter, often without pattern or prescription.

In Puglia's towns and villages, opportunities to interpret the idea of urbanism without effort abound along evolving streets and in public squares that maintain their core integrity. Does a bouncing

Figure 2-16: Trani: reading the dynamism of place.

Figure 2-17: Otranto: organic playspace.

ball against a venerable door suggest a model for certain types of urban playgrounds? Do windows open to the wind suggest building orientations that work? Do street vendors have lessons for evolving farmers' markets and "street food" back home? What provides a sense of safety in crowds, at all times of day?

These illustrative questions suggest the inspirational power of onsite personal experience, memorialized by imagery, as a basis for further analysis of diverse urban settings. But such inspiration and inquiry are only the beginning of adapting human-scale lessons to, for example, the younger, sometimes two-dimensional world of American urbanism, or the increasingly pervasive mixed-use redevelopment projects adjacent to transit hubs that seek a traditional neighborhood look and feel. What else is possible? Once this urbanism without effort is recognized, our streets and squares, beaches and byways all have a greater and unrealized multipurpose capacity, ripe for recalibration.

Factors Leading to Comfortable Community and Neighborhood

Corners

Street corners are an easy-to-observe element of the historical city and the transition from rural to urban. They are also a key component of the marriage of movement and settlement. The corner is one of the central places of urban life; even more so than public squares, which usually require a conscious set-aside of assembled space. Corners are an effortless and natural by-product of crossroads, the elemental feature of travel between places.

Figure 2-18: Karatu: a corner and commerce.

Figure 2-19: London: another corner and commerce.

In the planning, design, and real estate world, the "100 percent corner" is historic shorthand for flagship downtown locations—where the center of the action resides. As real estate, the corner is the most visible and accessible, therefore the most profitable, so we frequently find small corner stores punctuating neighborhoods and larger retail companies occupying corners in areas with more density and traffic volume.

In Australian country towns, hotels are frequent and prominent corner uses, often in "kitty corner" formation, as if to welcome travelers with multiple choices at key crossroads flanking town centers. Frequently, a prominent second-story veranda provides a dual-purpose, including outdoor space and outlooks for sleeping floor guests and shelter for entries, bars, and restaurants beneath.

Not only a pragmatic matter, the corner has been inspiration to authors and poets. Albert Camus noted the corner as among a city's

Figures 2-20 and 2-20A: Cobar, NSW, Australia, and the corner hotel, and Fremantle, Western Australia, adaptive reuse example.

most inventive places: "All great deeds and all great thoughts have a ridiculous beginning. Great works are often born on a street corner or in a restaurant's revolving door."[19]

Corners are by nature interdisciplinary, regardless of cultural surrounding. In *Tally's Corner*,[20] Elliott Liebow creates a memorable, human-scale chronicle of American inner-city life premised on the social order in and around a corner setting.

At crossroads, whether paved and straight or dirt and ill defined, destinations meet wheeled and other forms of transport, while natural systems meet reconstructed space. As modes of transportation coalesce, people watch and wait. Often, drainage, power, and other utilities focus at such central points, above and below ground. Corners are places of safety and intimidation, homogeneity and contrast. The corner also provides a vantage point and place of choice—here we pause to assess our surroundings before stepping off the curb or turning to follow the sidewalk.

Beyond the wry observation of Camus, urban corners may represent one of the best, most visible, and pragmatic opportunities to reorient our cities, and become nothing short of the baseline—the building blocks—for reinvention of city neighborhoods based on examples of what corners have symbolized, facilitated, and delineated since the first path crossed in an urban setting long ago.

Fusion Businesses

Fusion businesses can help replicate mixed neighborhoods and more typical effortless urbanism from the past. In my Seattle neighborhood, when a small outlet of a local ice cream business opened within the laundromat, it was visual evidence that creative enterprises bring originality and uniqueness, which also contribute to a sense of place.

My neighborhood is not alone. Consider Copenhagen's celebrated, multibranch Laundromat Café,[21] which has fused a food menu with laundry, and inspired a trend toward similar fusion cafes, such as San Francisco's Brain Wash.[22] These reinvented

Figures 2-21 and 2-21A: Seattle: the ice cream laundromat, night and day.

combinations of uses activate the area throughout the day and evening, as different functions take precedence at different times of the day, allowing both enhanced commerce and street life.

Land use regulations may need more flexibility in order to enable fusion businesses. Conventional zoning regulations often prohibit food service uses from operating beside more "industrial" uses such as laundries. In addition, such regulations often constrain placement of smaller start-up businesses within existing uses, and limit opportunities for walk-up windows or other flexible access.

Land use reform efforts can and should reinvent such conventional impediments to produce a more efficient, effortless, and compact city life and allow the flexibility of innovation and redefined urban traditions. As initial Seattle efforts illustrated, regulatory reforms aimed at reinvigorating more traditional and effortless development patterns into areas adjacent to single-family neighborhoods could be evolutionary rather than revolutionary, enabling a work environment where employment could be closer to home.[23] However, as height and scale allowances increased in return for affordable housing provision, it became clear to many that a "housing and livability agenda" had somehow exceeded the bounds of a comfortable, naturally occurring urbanism that is the focus here.

Many of today's efforts toward more sustainable cities, shared consumption lifestyles, and functional, multipurpose venues should be seen first as viable urbanism without effort, rather than indiscriminate application of popular ideas.

Perception of Safety in Nighttime Cities

If "cities, like cats, will reveal themselves at night,"[24] as the English poet Rupert Brooke suggests, is the nature of the city safe or unsafe in the urban darkness? Is a nighttime city better monitored and measured by crime statistics, rather than by human perception and poetry?

Figures 2-22 and 2-22A: Dublin and Florence: night perceptions.

In my view, Brooke's early twentieth-century poetry is a worthy start. His feline–city analogy provides a springboard for five important—and effortless—qualities of 24-hour, magnetic places. The first, safety, spurs four more—mobility, proximity, commerce, and interaction. We understand the benefits of these 24-hour places: legendary, all-night coding jags in the technology sector, spontaneous live performances, vibrant nightlife, and night markets, to name a few. All can act as impetus to enable a more robust evening public transit service and police presence, and the growing "night mayor" approaches inspired by Amsterdam's experience.[25]

The relationship between darkness and urbanism has been studied several times in interdisciplinary fashion, and at least one Massachusetts Institute of Technology course has been devoted to the "interaction design" of the associated "world of night."[26] However, my sense is that these efforts remain far more at the cutting edge than they should, given the importance of the 24-hour city as a symbol of urban vitality. Nighttime cities may start with the romantic sentiment that they are effortless—in reality, specific attention to perception of safety may be required to implement what begins with simple inspiration.

In discussion of public safety issues concerning urban areas, law enforcement, design, and planning often remain in their respective silos, devoid of integration. Ongoing neighborhood policing and social service initiatives should be more explicitly integrated with the renewed focus on environmental and urban design criteria for safe streetscapes.

Concepts of Crime Prevention Through Environmental Design (CPTED)—frequently international in nature[27]—have been present for decades and were implied in Jane Jacobs's work. For example, certain CPTED principles have been instituted along neighborhood tram lines in Melbourne, Australia, including ample (glare-protective) night lighting; territorial sensitivities to illuminated, sidewalk-oriented window areas; enhancement of the role of passing vehicles; transparent protection from weather at building entries; and low bushes or lower picket-type fencing along the street to limit access while allowing for entry visibility.

Figure 2-23: Melbourne: sidewalk dining with overhead protection.

Similar safety-enhancement approaches for safety of female transit users have received wide attention.[28] Many cities and civic associations have also advocated for integration of CPTED principles.[29]

Increased advocacy efforts for funding of pedestrian and bicycle infrastructure will accelerate policy and regulation encouraging such principles for safety. This should lead to further discussion opportunities for "complete streets," including the dimension of lighting to facilitate wider, multimodal use over a longer percentage of the day.

If evening light and crowds merge to create a sense of safety, if walking and transit define mobility and proximity, and if commerce goes on once the sun sets, then human interaction with the

Figure 2-23A: Saint-Raphaël: the dimension of lighting in action.

built environment can extend the urbanism without effort called for here.

The Comfort of Sustainable Storefronts

Across the world, vital storefronts are a universal indicator of urban success, while empty businesses are akin to the ruins of Pompeii. Even when storefronts go empty, some cities find ways to simulate that all is well, as if to emulate more classic, effortless urbanism.

False facades, community art, allowance for temporary "pop-up" shops, and the look and feel of a vibrant business district often substitute for empty spaces through glass.

Figures 2-24 and 2-24A: Cairns and Porto: traditional storefronts, in context.

There are authentic lessons to be learned from smaller towns, where commercial districts show remnants of what was.

Photographs of the remaining skeleton of Bovill, Idaho's downtown area illustrate what we now seek in bigger places—compact, mixed-use blocks with character—and communicate memories of the effortless dynamism between the neighborhood grocery and the watering spot next door. In Bovill, several buildings are proudly engraved "1914." I believe that if those buildings were airlifted to my Seattle neighborhood in 2018, they would fit in just fine.

The old, naturally occurring storefront may now be scarcer in the hinterlands, but it has found new life as one of the building blocks of the reinvented city, where neighborhood areas are increasingly more flexibly zoned to allow more mixed uses than in the past. Such mixed uses and associated proximity are primary contributors to complete streets, social interaction, walkable neighborhoods, and transit-oriented central places. The passion for such "first-floor retail" has been declared and codified in planning goals and land use regulations alike.

Figure 2-25: Bovill, Idaho: downtown that today's city wants.

In Rockville Town Center in Rockville, Maryland, storefront design guidelines are typical of such emphasis and further encourage creativity in how storefronts present to the street:

> Rockville's "great urban place" sets the stage upon which the storefronts will be layered. Because of the investment in quality for all aspects of Rockville Town Center, storefront guidelines encourage creative and well-designed individual expressions of tenant identity. Strong urban storefronts are essential in the creation of an attractive and exciting, dining, shopping, and leisure environment.[30]

Highly evolved cities now seem to rise above the status quo by seamlessly implementing a timeless and universal urban characteristic in a local context, seizing opportunities that have worked before to create the magnetism of success.

However, the romance of an idea can be offset by urban process and politics—and risks re-creating the unsustainable place where passersby ask pedestrians if there is a store in the neighborhood. Recognizing such risks, in Seattle, a regulatory reform roundtable recommended that certain street-level retail requirements be relaxed to avoid more empty spaces in challenging times.[31] The city council enacted only some of the recommendations, as the reality of politics interceded.

Storefronts have always made the city, and as economic challenges continue, more flexibility to create dynamic and interesting street uses should remain at the forefront of city-making—mindful of flexibility necessary to facilitate the latent city rhythm that businesses need to survive.

Furthering the Innate People–Place Relationships Based on the Human Experience

The elements of this chapter present a broad range of observable, naturally occurring relationships between humans and the urban environment. How can we recognize and fully understand exam-

Figure 2-26: Sydney: Glebe neighborhood and the Australian vital commercial front: security above, protection from the elements, and pedestrian space adjacent to storefronts, separate from cars.

ples of this de facto urbanism without effort from personal observation of these relationships in action? Which examples of urbanism without effort might be best remembered in urban diaries that document how we relate to the surrounding city? How can we better assure that these examples will be adapted to other settings in ways that fit local circumstances? The next chapter profiles some ideal applications of the innate human–city relationships described here, focusing on elements such as public open space, adaptive reuse, first principles of movement and settlement, and human perception of urban surroundings.

Successful examples of urbanism without effort should foster the creativity and initiative of city residents and avoid "one size fits all" marketing strategies and solutions. Chapters 3 and 4 further discuss this process for contextual evaluation, reuse, and adaptation.

Chapter 3

Capturing the Best Urban Diary Examples

FOLLOWING THE APPROACH OF THE URBAN DIARY discussed in chapter 2, and expanded upon in *Seeing the Better City*, this chapter presents reflective vignettes of varying lengths, based on my collection of photographs and observations of local and international examples. These vignettes demonstrate how urbanism without effort is premised on common human affinities and varied in expression by cultural context, historical circumstance, and other unique factors, such as geography and climate. They demonstrate the challenges of creating livable cities that are universal and timeless, and how solutions require careful observation in the context of local circumstances.

The vignettes should act as a catalyst to spur education, creative policy-making tools, and thoughtful reflection by individuals compiling their own urban diaries or seeking a more complete understanding of city life. Surely, the challenges of how to implement ideas presented in each of the following vignettes could generate books, articles, and lengthy debates in and of themselves, far beyond the scope of this work. In my case, *Seeing the Better City* provides a next step in applying related tools and techniques beyond the examples set out here.

The vignettes are not prescriptive, nor are they intended as dictated policies or other forms of prescribed messaging. Rather, I include them to illustrate and inspire, as they are, at minimum, photogenic with a compelling narrative. They also provide an opportunity for ground-up understanding and consensus about how each vignette's core ideas might be authentically reapplied elsewhere.

In summary, this chapter offers a "don't try this at home" approach,[1] predicated upon carefully ground-truthing the adaptability of a chosen example of successful urbanism. Any new policy, planning initiative, regulatory reform, or other implementation should first consider the historical, geographical, environmental, cultural, and political contexts presented within each vignette.

Vignette 1: The Inherently Walkable

Walkability is at the center of today's placemaking and the search for healthier, more sustainable communities. Significant advocacy, research, professional activities, and governmental policy making are now devoted to increasing opportunities to walk in—and between—cities and towns. Yet I have concluded, as a result of observations abroad and many discussions with walkability advocates, that an emphasis on urban walking resonates best as a first principle of human life. It is significant to both the marriage of movement and settlement (land use and transportation) and the blending of traditional urban conduct highlighted in chapter 2 as an innate relationship related to urbanism without effort.

Figure 3-1: Laetoli Track at Oldupai: fun snapshot, important walk.

East Africa provides a surprising urban diary entry, based on a stereotypical museum display of arguably the world's first walkable place, the 3.75-million-year-old fossilized footprints of the Laetoli track near Oldupai Gorge, Tanzania.[2] Laetoli underpins the universal dynamic of movement and settlement that matured in villages, towns, and cities. At Laetoli and Oldupai, the germination of crossroads, corners, and the inherently walkable place is obvious. The modern urbanist's search to fulfill desires for "walkability" is rooted here.

One of the best examples of the inherently walkable is the Italian *passeggiata*, a time-honored tradition that takes advantage of the compact, vibrant cities and towns of the Adriatic and Mediterranean. Not only a basis for exercise, taking a walk is ultimately both a family-oriented and a social event, a chance to reconnect with friends and neighbors, and to see and be seen. As Dr. Richard Jackson has noted in *Designing Healthy Communities*,[3] it is reflective of organic place, and an indicator of a healthy practice that occurred in historic built environments that came into existence long before motorized transport.

The term "passeggiata" is, in fact, literally translated as both movement (a walk and a stroll) and a component of settlement (a public walk or promenade). It demarcates the end of the workday, enhances health, and historically provided an integral sense of community at the levels of family and town. Travel writers invite tourists to participate, not only for touristic exploration but for immersion in medieval tradition, courtship, and other sociopolitical aspects of urban life first learned in the interactions of strolling and mingling en route to piazzas.[4]

Figure 3-2: Otranto passeggiata.

For our purposes, the *passeggiata* is an inspirational example of urbanism without effort and provides simultaneous expression of cultural attributes and coveted urban behavior. But how much does its naturally occurring success depend on climate and the endemic culture that created both the tradition and its facilitating, usually historical, infrastructure?

The holistic, cultural, and physical nature of the *passeggiata* illuminates the context issue discussed throughout this book and leads directly to whether the cultural nuances of the Italian evening stroll readily translate across the world. Can we achieve in Cheyenne, Wyoming, or Nordic climates, what occurs naturally in Siena, Italy? How can we best present inspirational examples that emulate indigenous tradition without overstepping the bounds of reality as forewarned long ago by Huxtable, and discussed in chapter 2?

Figure 3-2A: Stockholm in winter, a Nordic "passeggiata" on a frozen lake?

The innate characteristics of the *passeggiata* are particularly suitable for the tool of the urban diary. The inherent vitality of the activity lends itself to photography or video and illustrates the cultural tradition and the unique and distinguishable aspects of place. In summary, rather than prescribe a walkable place outright, why not stop short of cause-oriented recruitment and sweeten the prospect with illustration of the effortless nature of such places?

Comprehensive answers lie in analysis of local context, including the prospects for pedestrian plan and policy development and in solutions that range from additional educational efforts to infrastructure improvements (e.g., crosswalks, sidewalks) and safety campaigns.

Vignette 2: Convertible, People-Oriented Spaces

Convertible people-oriented spaces, such as Barcelona's partially reengineered Las Ramblas,[5] and more naturally occurring public urban squares like Rome's Campo de' Fiori[6] accommodate a range of different activities and uses throughout a 24-hour period—from market, crossroads of commerce, and dining center by day to social congregating point both day and night, while presenting multiple elements of history and changing use over time.

These spaces often incorporate *passeggiata* elements or destinations and can easily serve as exemplary spaces for the innate relationships characteristic of urbanism without effort, particularly the interplay of factors leading to comfortable community and neighborhood and related collaboration and safety.

Often, to evoke the vision of an urbanist future, we reflect on images of public spaces borne of a sociocultural tradition, like Campo de' Fiori. However, given the current generational and marketplace tilt toward such walkable, compact, mixed-use experiences, are we deluding ourselves by presuming a Campo de' Fiori experience could be applied to every American city? In reality it might be something dramatically out of context.

Figure 3-3: Barcelona: Plaça de Catalunya "occupied."

Figure 3-4: Barcelona: the Ramblas style.

Figure 3-5: Rome: the quintessential urban space, Campo de' Fiori.

My own, filmed walks through Campo de' Fiori and nearby Piazza Navona at night display the magical confluence of place, commerce, human social activity, conducive climate, and sense of safety.[7] The historic story of the place itself suggests that the context in which a place evolves is key to the actual physical experience and its related urban character. Do we do injustice to a rich history of place by assuming we can re-create the physical form inherent in the "backstory" of a specific place? For example, a former field, once the location of gallows for minor offenses; a juncture of streets surprisingly devoted to trades; a market by day then later a haven of nightlife. Can a newly created place be just as rich in experience without its own backstory?

Some years ago, while on sabbatical from my former law firm, I presented a talk asking Cornell University students who were studying in Rome to reflect on the context of what they had learned while studying abroad. A summary of the handout appears as follows, which contains a proposition that could very well have originated from a client requesting legal assistance through my law practice.

> Rome contains some of the world's most successful "public spaces." Assume you are an American planning director who receives a request from a city council member who has just returned from a trip to Rome. The council member wants to pressure local mall redevelopers to create a space reminiscent of Campo de' Fiori at the center of a 1960's era shopping mall which is subject to pending development approvals for a multi-million-dollar renovation. What features can you insert in the development agreement draft to attempt such ambiance? Can successful public spaces be successfully legislated?

The issue of context dominated the questions asked in the handout. Similarly, context is key to the dilemma of imposing patterns from another history on an urban setting derived from a different cultural tradition. As with the *passeggiata*, this dilemma may yield more questions than certainty in changing times.

Certainly, such spaces are ripe for first-person observation and inspiration. But should professionals indiscriminately design and program local spaces that only mimic the authentic or original spaces? Should every city have a "High Line" or other reuse of abandoned or now-dysfunctional infrastructure such as an unused ramp or tunnel? Is replication possible without resulting in Huxtable's Disney-fication, or is it even wise?

Perhaps the answer lies in the scale of the endeavor and my oft-repeated distinction between inspiration and prescriptive replication. Assuming such an idea is well vetted and public input is under way, review of the linked videos mentioned earlier could be used as an "idea management" step to assess the adaptability of an active Campo de' Fiori–type space. I have written about such idea management before, from the standpoint of a practitioner, anchored on the "how" to implement new approaches in cities, and I have suggested careful and contextual due diligence before presentation of visions that risk repudiation and rancor. In this case, rather than prescribe the qualities of the European square, why not display outright the possibilities inherent in naturally occurring city life as an "idea management" tool[8] to assess the realistic value associated with local adoption?

Vignette 3: Building Community

A spontaneous summer evening gathering in a Seattle neighborhood alley reaffirmed my belief that real neighborhood experiences can provide a meaningful gloss on current discussions about how to make cities better and increase the benefits of shared places for all. This led to my position that the best urbanism is that which

Figure 3-6: Seattle: alley movie night.

is already there, waiting to be nurtured; accordingly, this vignette became the original inspiration for this book.

These successful neighborhood experiences are based on key innate relationships between humans and the urban environment (see chapter 2), which depend on an interplay of factors leading to comfortable community and neighborhood and the related collaboration and safety without significant government intervention.

How it happened: one Saturday night, in response to an email invitation that was unrelated to any city-sponsored program or effort of any organized community group, I went to the movies by walking 100 feet from my home. Admission was free. And it was not in the comfort of an isolated home or downtown space, but among some 20 neighbors in an everyday place, hidden and in plain sight: Monica and Michael's alley entry, against Anne and Jerry's retaining wall.

Figure 3-7: Seattle: building the organic theater.

Our last summer "alley movie night" was an important reminder that a city neighborhood can experience community without prescription. In the spirit of organic examples from history and the two-dimensional perspective of the city recollected in Jackson's "Discovery of the Street" (as introduced in chapter 1), this urbanism without effort was as natural as the organic *passeggiata* and contextually authentic, unimposed, and self-defined.

We can try awfully hard—sometimes too hard, in my opinion—to proselytize and debate ideas and opportunities for the city as though inventing them for the first time, without acknowledging instances in which the urbanism we already have can act as a precursor, leading the way.

In particular, the general potential for American urban alleys remains in the spotlight. This attention, which is often aspirational, is well deserved given the raw alley palette for remade narrow streets reminiscent of the organic European tradition already discussed: pedestrian in scale, interesting, and a natural focus for greening street life and new small businesses.

Many other essays (e.g., Alyse Nelson writing in *Sightline*[9]) have recalled alleys' placemaking role within the urbanist toolbox. Specific, grant-funded work by Seattle's Daniel Toole (including his self-published book, *Tight Urbanism*[10]) has emphasized the now-iconic reclaimed laneway precedent of Melbourne, Australia—where underused spaces between downtown buildings were given new commercial and artistic life—and beyond.

As in the case of other vignettes, so far, the capacity for first-person inspiration and inspirational aspects of reclaimed alleys requires no further discussion. The challenges, of course, come from programmatic and policy eligibility and implementation.

It would be easy for city staff to collate existing instances of activities like alley movie night in updates to visioning or planning documents (which was suggested after one of my recent speaking engagements on the topic); but how to fund reclaiming and maintaining these alleys? And, as with many instances of infrastruc-

Figure 3-8: Melbourne: a classic laneway scene.

ture improvement, we must determine where and how the private sector can make a difference in implementing improvements and maintenance too costly for today's municipal public transportation and utility agencies. After all, it's not just about clearing away the dumpsters. As I've noted before (on Seattle's KUOW radio[11]), public rights-of-way, stormwater system maintenance, pavement resurfacing, and other forms of street improvement may be required in order to materially reinvent desired space.

Admittedly, not all of us have traditional alleys at our back doors (which we often treat as main entries), but those of us who do can readily avail ourselves of the once and future urbanism of alley reinvention. Those of us who don't might find that a driveway and garage suffice for now, or catalog in urban diaries similar instances of neighborhood-based urbanism without effort that have stood the test of time.

Email, potluck food and drink, equipment setup, and a bedsheet-as-movie-screen can transform public space into a community gathering point, not because of doctrine or dogma, but because it is as natural as seeking out affiliation with the people who live in the place next door.

Vignette 4: Fundamentals of Land Use and Transport: Shelter and the Wheel

Just as Laetoli and Oldupai in vignette 1 provided the inadvertent baseline for walking, paths, crossroads, and corners, other examples in Tanzania strip away the complexities of Western culture to expose the simplicity of human needs and relationship to surroundings. Both rural and urban examples indicate fundamental relationships between land use, transportation, and the surrounding environment in developing countries, not unlike the innate relationships between humans and cities discussed in chapter 2.

Particularly noteworthy are the basic dwelling structures, the frequency of pedestrian travel, and the widespread commercial use of bicycles, generally no longer seen in areas of the world where the motorized vehicle is prevalent. This vignette contains observations relating to the precursors of city life and urbanism without effort—true first principles—that further an understanding of the most fundamental human needs.

At the juxtaposition of tradition, tourism, and sustainability, these dramatic photographs tell a story that is hardly apparent at first glance. Only a stone's throw from the traffic and diversity of Arusha, Tanzania, village communities—what we might call neighborhoods—are preserved in the distinctly nonurban, tribal traditions that still overlay portions of East Africa.

Figure 3-9: Ngorongoro: Maasai village.

Visitors passing through the Ngorongoro Conservation Area[12] into the Serengeti Plain will easily discern Maasai[13] villages—distinctive settlements and cultural attributes of the country's oft-noted tribe—dotting the landscape. Cows, central to Maasai measures of wealth and marriage worthiness, are abundant, as are boldly colored robes, talking sticks, and spears—all on display as tribal members take long walks across varied terrain.

Roadside Maasai observers, whether solo or in groups, help define the travel experience from Arusha to safari destinations. Safari-bound visitors take note and wave, and sometimes people from this contrasting culture of Land Cruisers stop to take a photo or to buy local jewelry and crafts. In such interactions, traditions converge, as both the musical expressions of the Maasai culture and the negotiations of modern commerce play their respective roles.

This visual and interactive experience is compelling, if not overwhelming, and it is not difficult to romanticize the storybook Africa

Figure 3-10: Ngorongoro: "neighborhood."

we want to see. Nonetheless, the landscape presents issues that are important and relevant to naturally occurring urbanism when contrasted with modern approaches to land use issues.

The confluence of age-old tradition and the evolving acceptance of modern technology and culture in East African settlements led me to a review of comparative "then and now" photographs of Brainerd, Minnesota, presented by Chuck Marohn in his early writing for his national advocacy movement, Strong Towns.[14] One photograph, as summarized by Marohn, showed a vital 1890s street scene bustling with urban life at a time "without zoning, design standards, tax-increment financing, local economic development initiatives and the automobile." In stark contrast, a photograph from the same location today showed an empty, windswept street.

Brainerd, as presented, became the perfect foil for a nagging question brought home from Tanzania—the same question posed from the outset of this book: do we sometimes regulate away the urban vitality of our cities by attempting complex, prescriptive fixes—aimed at modeling or reclaiming what used to evolve naturally—and ironically squelch first principles of human shelter and transportation?

Inherited forms of shelter and age-old methods of transportation are to residential zoning and infrastructure planning what oral histories were to Gutenberg—the backdrop of rich tradition for codification and institutional creation. If safety and well-being are maintained, such institutionalization may be laudable for preserving practices or legends otherwise lost with time.

However, if the result is lost functionality, needless complexity, discrimination, or prohibitive expense, the institution may need reexamination. For instance, what if a zoning code is no longer

Figure 3-11: Ngorongoro: Maasai village.

cohesive, or it impedes rather than accomplishes societal goals? What if the automobile is overused, at increasing expense, when a bicycle, cart, or other transportation would do, with the added value of better health and more exercise?

Sometimes the contrast of a different place and tradition can refocus priorities and enhance the senses, much like the urbanism without effort of alley movie night. It becomes a mandatory addition to the urban diary.

For example, consider the iconic Maasai village, with a perimeter of brush to discourage animal invasion and a central open space for market or celebration. Consider further the adjacent huts built of dung and sticks with cramped entry spaces and "room" division with spaces little more in size than our natural reach.

I learned by visiting such a village and conferring with the son of the chief that the straightforward form and function work, as they

Figure 3-12: Ngorongoro: Maasai village.

have for countless generations. Observing this naturally occurring, straightforward life was a lesson in the risks of prescriptive, out-of-context solutions. It seemed outrageous to think of such fundamental village configurations in land use regulatory terms, that is, to "zone" this tradition, with pedantic setbacks, ratios, heights, and densities, or to fall prey to legislation increasing dimensional allowances based on cultural "metrics," such as number of livestock owned.

Consider also the traditional forms of transportation used when a car is unavailable, inaccessible, or inappropriate. Commerce and people can move without regulation. Wheels and the human body go places in ways we have often forgotten. Innovative, human-propelled transport, often with goods attached, knows no bounds.

Figure 3-13: Karatu: the basic wheel.

Figure 3-14: Karatu: more wheel basics.

But, in such situations, what if regulations required paint striping of "use pathways" where it is most convenient to travel? Or outlawed the simple wheeled vehicles shown above, which are sometimes the most functional purveyors of here to there? What if government regulation attempted to limit the weight of what can be carried by hand or cart?

When these questions are posed and we also contemplate zoning classifications such as IH-1 (Indigenous Hut 1), CAR (Cow–Area Ratio), or monikers such as MMCW (Multimodal Carts and Wheelbarrows), the dialogue sounds absurd. And that may be the very point.

Marohn's Brainerd, Minnesota, then and now, coupled with observed imagery from the developing world, implies that through the complex evolution of initially well-meaning institutionalization, perhaps we risk losing our way.

I suggest that we reassess—with simplicity and a more effortless urbanism in mind—and recall Mumford's movement and settlement paradigm expressed as the first principles of shelter and the wheel.

Vignette 5: Cities, Sustained and Evolved

Chapter 2 explained the importance of sustainability, defined as the organic mixture of built and natural environments, and how the building blocks of the sustainable city can combine over time to produce innate, seamless, and effortless relationships, including the adaptive reuse of the built environment at an urban scale. This two-part vignette provides considerable detail and comparative context about two European models that best explain the principles set out in chapter 2.

One compelling example of a sustainable (failed, but recently renewed) mixture of the built and natural environments can be seen in the story of the sassi of Matera, Italy. Another, unrivaled example of adaptive reuse comes from Diocletian's Palace in Split, Croatia. The discussion that follows, of both cities, provides inspiration, application of urbanism without effort principles, and suggested guidance for policy and implementation.

The Sustainable City of Stone

Today, in the provinces of southeastern Italy, the landscape is changing as a new world of alternative energy infrastructure blends insular hill towns, turbines, and solar panels across traditional farmland. Yet, on the same horizons, other, age-old reflections of once-effortless local sustainable practices echo time-honored human traditions as lessons for urban reinvention in a networked world.

Figure 3-15: Matera's sassi.

On the surface, daily urban life appears resilient, perhaps an attribute most notable among strolling, night crowds in the public realm of the traditional *passeggiata*. Urbanism without effort exists amid commerce and touristic curiosity, along streets, beside buildings, and as a component of cross-town strolls discussed in vignette 1. These striking examples of authentic urban life appear in many forms—from venerable town centers to children playing in the streets—in often spontaneous and random fashion.

Matera, a city of approximately 60,000 located in Basilicata, Italy, has a legacy that frames a remarkable setting of almost 10,000 years of continuous human occupation and adaptation. Its unique history of urban ecology, from sustainability to squalor, inspired UNESCO to designate it a World Heritage Site,[15] and its old Jerusalem-like aura has attracted several movie directors, including Mel Gibson for his movie *The Passion of the Christ*. Matera's legacy is also

Figure 3-16: Matera: public realm.

a place setting precedent for the sustainable city, as described in chapter 2's reference to the summary of sustainable city characteristics by Harvard professor Joan Busquets, particularly as to long-term integration of natural geography and water systems.

In keeping with the Brundtland Report, also summarized earlier, a sustainable model must be resilient in the face of population expansion, new economies, and politics in order to stand the test of time. UNESCO has repeatedly used Matera as an educational case study for the sustainable city in local context. An associated Baltic Sea Project educational guide for "observing and innovating urban ecology" (portions of which are summarized here) laments how Matera's sustainability depended on its isolation and champions its local examples as inspiration.

Ironically, Matera's focal point, the sassi (literally "stones") cliff dwellings, are not readily apparent on entering the town today.

They are hidden, essentially as artifacts, in two urban valleys adjacent to an ancient, cave-hewn riverbed below the modern city. Yet, in their time, the sassi were an exemplar of sustainable practices with a textbook marriage of habitation, infrastructure, and ecosystem.

The sassi of Matera invite observation, immersion, and study of the town as a holistic artifact of evolved sustainability. The sassi include dwellings that successfully adapted to both a cool, moist winter climate and hot, dry summers. Their story is one of systems integration and efficient infrastructure—the use of natural (later extended) cliff dwelling caves for food storage, housing, and urban social and commercial functions. Cisterns, built into the rock underneath such dwellings, collected channeled rainwater, resulting in nonpolluted freshwater that was successfully preserved in winter for year-round use.

As a largely self-sufficient settlement of 10,000–20,000 inhabitants leading into and beyond the Middle Ages, Matera grew its

Figure 3-17: Matera as artifact.

own food supply—nearby gardens were located on the rooftop of the next cliff dwelling or the one below. Waste, wastewater, and manure were recycled. Building material consisted of the local chalk-like sandstone (*tuffa*), and building stone was perpetually re-created from inner extension of the caves into the cliffs. In Matera's sustainable world, there was little need for significant means of transportation other than to and from nearby agricultural lands; therefore, the urban form remained largely unchanged until the eighteenth century.

Then, as a result of widespread trade revival, Matera became less isolated, and the sustainable systems management that had made it successful for so long broke down. New residents brought over-population to Matera and overcrowding of the sassi. The water collection system became fouled by the use of cisterns as dwellings for less privileged inhabitants. As water use increased, the capacity to safely conserve it was lost. Animals lived in close quarters with humans, and waste management systems lost integrity. In the end, the trade and commerce of an emerging capitalist world undid Matera.

Figure 3-18: Matera retrofitted today.

Through the advocacy of Carlo Levi's post–World War II writing,[16] Matera's poor and crowded living conditions, low life expectancy, high infant mortality rates, and disease infestation became well known. Government intervention forced abandonment of the sassi and the relocation of over 15,000 inhabitants until the 1990s. Architect Pietro Laureano—known for expertise in the urban ecology of the sassi—championed the sassi's legacy of sustainability and adaptation to the local environment, and by 1996, Matera received its UNESCO World Heritage Site designation. In the time since, the sassi have been and continue to be retrofitted. Today, renewed residential, commercial, and touristic life is readily apparent.

As the Baltic Sea Project study urged, the local sustainability solutions of Matera provide a vital example for today's more complex world. By implication, the closed, historical nature of Matera's past might not be reproducible today. Nonetheless, the study recounts the Matera story in a manner that is valuable here, referencing the uniqueness of local context and example.

> The sustainable town of Matera from the past showed a balanced ecology based on low consumption of local resources and recycling. Almost no materials or food came from abroad, trade and transport was extremely limited to the surrounding agricultural land and based on land transport done by animals or people. This transport constituted at the same time the communication lines. Muscular power and wood for fire, oil for light were the scarce energy sources used. The town stayed literally unchanged and independent of external supply through hundreds of years, with very little growth in population.
>
> Its decline as sustainable habitation came . . . because of rapid immigration in a period (18th Century) of growing World trade.
>
> During the last two centuries, neither the basic population nor the political [sic] powerful landowners, traders or governors wanted

the sustainability and independency continued. They wanted to profit from the market. . . .

In many countries, planners and entrepreneurs have developed local urban technology, mostly green housing, zero energy buildings, electric transport systems, but also urban ecology projects for a full-scale towns [*sic*] or suburbs, though still local solutions. . . .

Nevertheless local solutions have shown a variety of options, and the importance of using local ideas, resources and materials is inevitable. It is simply one of the fundamental components of urban ecology, as well as it is a strategy "to break through the barriers" for unsustainable urban development.[17]

Figure 3-19: Matera overview.

Can the principles of Matera be successfully applied to cities today, where regional, national, and world markets impact local autonomy and economy like never before? Contemporary discussion of sustainable cities seems to assume modern equivalents for Matera's local systems, including carbon-neutrality goals and tool-based approaches to transportation, water, waste, power and communication systems, energy districts, rainwater collection, urban agriculture, bioswales, and innovative architectural approaches, to name but a few.

In my view, we now attempt to re-create the golden age of Matera on a wide, sometimes indiscriminate scale, couched in language of inspiration rather than precedent. Yet the sustainable cities we seek should incorporate qualities from Matera and other documented human traditions that are readily ascertainable, recordable, and eligible for inspirational presentation. Experiencing both the physical remains of sustainable Matera and the ongoing repopulation of the sassi today provides yet another example of the urbanism that is already in our midst, ripe for adaptation.

The Palace Adapts to a City

In contexts beyond Matera's unique story, can we use urbanism without effort principles to imagine or project how the city of tomorrow will reflect adaptive reuse of the city of today? I don't think we ask that question broadly enough, and our day-to-day, property-specific incrementalism easily overshoots the greatest organic development lessons from history in favor of today's city politics, regulation, and economic constraints.

How did our predecessors address similar transitions of buildings and neighborhoods when reuse was a cost-based practical necessity? What usually came next? What can we learn from those stories? When surroundings evolve, we should consider, as with Matera, whether we can create incentives and inspiration for transformational places that are sustainable in form and function and based on reuse of past sociocultural and physical foundations.

Figure 3-20: Split: Diocletian's Palace. (Credit: Comparative aerial photo from Wikipedia under a Creative Commons license)

Figure 3-21: Split: adaptable reuse at an urban scale. (Credit: Comparative aerial photo from Wikipedia under a Creative Commons license)

When considering questions related to transition from old to new, I believe the focus should sharply embrace Alexander's "natural city," Rykwert's "fabric," and "the artifact-based focus" that he shares with historians: the multifaceted evolution of a neighborhood or the city as a whole is more than the particular buildings themselves. In this regard, one city, Split, Croatia (another UNESCO World Heritage site[18]), is deserving of a very hard look premised upon how it evolved.

Amid Split's old town center, within and next to the ruins of the retirement palace of the Roman emperor Diocletian, adaptive reuse is observable at an urban scale—a place that began as something completely different from what it is today lives on anew, in another age—more juxtaposition than reinvention.

I first visited Split in 1968, when it was part of the old Yugoslavia, and returned many times in the years that followed. There, the survival and reuse of historic elements tells a valuable tale of

Figure 3-22: Split: the cardo.

sustainability in the style of Busquets's "historic city," with lessons learned regarding the human capacity to reuse and adapt the built environment to current needs.

Shortly after AD 300, on the site of Split's town center, workers completed Diocletian's Palace. Diocletian was the first Roman emperor to voluntarily abdicate (possibly for medical reasons) and retire in the modern sense; he viewed the palace as a purposeful respite from power, aptly located in his home region.

After Diocletian's death, the palace became a refuge for exiled imperial family members. Then, through serendipity, after the Avars and Slavs destroyed the nearby Roman city of Salona at the beginning of the seventh century, the palace became a shelter for fleeing citizens. Later, it became a medieval town, then a Renaissance regional center. Somewhat surprisingly, it eventually became a major city—with core elements of the palace still prominent today.

The spirit of Split is best captured in Thomas Swick's essay "Croatian Pop"[19] (a dynamic newspaper article later reprinted in *The Best American Travel Writing, 2001*). His poetic vent rivals the best descriptions of active public places.

> I slid through more right-angled alleys that deposited me into an hallucination: a sunken square hemmed in by antiquities. The delicate remains of a colonnade filigreed one side, and the skeletal façade of a temple, now buttressed by brick. . . . Spotlights dramatized the age-blackened columns, giving the scene a crumbling magnificence, while the cafe tables spread across the peristyle provided a jarring contemporary note. So that welded onto the indoor/outdoor motif—niches and statuary under the stars—was the even more compelling one of ancient and modern: teenagers flirting on ruinous walls; couples drinking in the shadow of the gods. It was like stumbling upon a cocktail party in the Roman Forum.

How did this scene come into being? In essence, the palace, which spanned almost 10 acres, contained enough elements of classical urbanity—including the gridded crossroads of a military camp (the ancient *castrum* and its standard roads, the *decumanus* and *cardo*), as well as several ceremonial spaces and religious structures—so that when it repopulated after the destruction of Salona, it became easily adaptable to what we now consider "urban uses."

This unintentional convertibility shows an interesting evolution of

- a mausoleum into a cathedral;
- the *cardo* into a winding medieval street that remains today;
- the crossing of the *decumanus* and *cardo* at the peristyle (a classical courtyard below the emperor's apartments) into a baptistry, public square, and historic urban center; and
- the emperor's apartments into the structural framework of a residential area.

Due to the interesting transformation of the palace into a city, Split has drawn visitors for hundreds of years. In 1764, the Scottish architect Robert Adam profiled Split's unrivaled preservation of Roman architecture through collected drawings,[20] that were often acknowledged as inspiration for the Georgian architectural tradition of parts of London, Bath, and Bristol.

In the last century, many excavations and publications that followed by local and American teams have admirably documented the palace's history and transformation (including the often-cited work of the brothers Jerko and Tomas Marasović, whom I had the honor of meeting as a teenager). In their writings,[21] the Marasovićs advocated a universal message in the context of continuing investigation, discovery, and restoration, "ensuring . . . renewed function within the context of a modern urban community."

While Split guidebook references contain cursory summaries of the palace's history, the confluence of past and present discussed here is not often mentioned in the American dialogue, nor is it consistently cited as prospective learning for cities around the world. This is a missed opportunity.

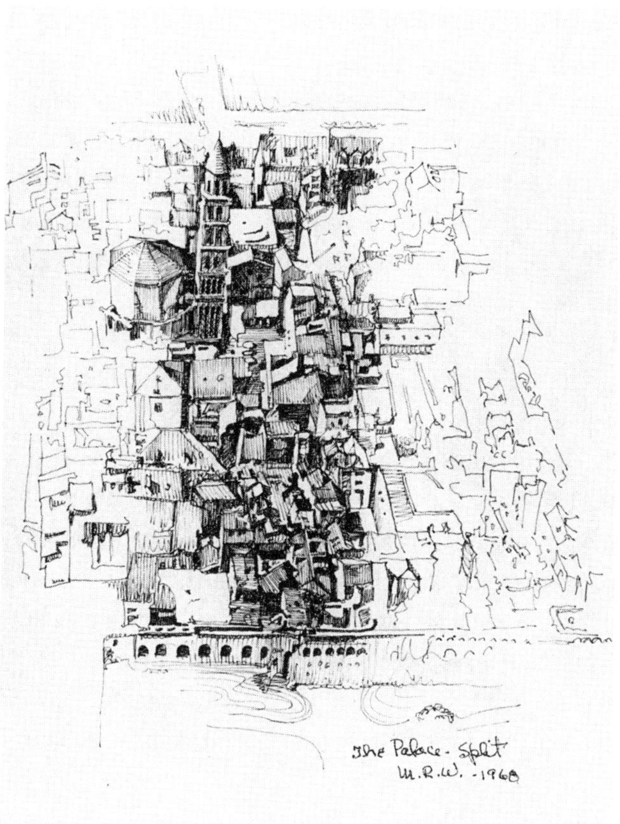

Figure 3-23: A depiction of Split's organic overlay.

I believe that visiting Diocletian's Palace and reflecting on how the old can blend with the new provides incomparable perspective, which could add value to today's discussion of familiar building restoration approaches. It could even influence already innovative, largely replacement-style redevelopment of areas like former military facilities on Treasure Island in San Francisco, an airport (e.g., the former Stapleton Airport in Denver), multiple former mental hospital institutional campuses, or the repurposed St. Luke's Hospital in Cleveland. The scale of adaptation in Split confirms how humans can be at home and enriched by large-scale incorporation of the past.

A *National Geographic* summary of Split hints at potential lessons:

> The result? Gothic and Renaissance buildings incorporating the Roman remnants into their relatively "modern" styles, all within the palace's original walls . . . [more] recently, that hodgepodge of ancient structures has been repurposed yet again to become today's trendy cafés, bars, and boutiques—a hub of neon and bustling crowds and window-shopping delights.[22]

Split is one of those places best understood firsthand, to fully realize the true experience of place and to witness how people live, work, and entertain while integrating the history around them. However, short of an actual visit, several of Peter Watts's 360-degree photographs at the Panoramic Earth website substantially simulate the experience,[23] in the form of a three-dimensional urban diary that aptly complements Swick's essay. Family life exists amid shops, restaurants, and bars, with more recently added wayfinding signs summarizing venues at the head of narrow streets.

Swick continues his first-person narrative in "Croatian Pop":

> But what really distinguishes the complex today is not its size or its symmetries but its fantastic utilitarianism. It is not just that people now gather where Praetorian Guards once strolled, but that they live here. In what must stand as one of the world's, if not first, at least most spectacular instances of adaptive reuse, the citizens of Split blithely built their dwellings within the palace. They grafted their humble residences onto the walls and filled in the arcades with bedroom windows. Just as weeds sprout among ruins in other lands, here it's houses. (It is almost as if, after the Cultural Revolution, the Chinese had erected apartment blocks in the Forbidden City.) . . . I would stroll the grounds shaking my head in wonderment at the curtained front doors next to erstwhile temples, the soccer balls sailing past toppled pillars. I could not walk along the waterfront promenade without staring up in amazement at the stately columns embedded in the condo façade, and occasionally bookending sagging lines of wash.[24]

In other cities, some historic urban cores still survive, and there are many examples of these—from Istanbul to Venice to Jerusalem—even Dubrovnik. Old towns, often within formerly defensive walls, became functional, large-scale artifacts, some evolved urban areas and some tourist meccas. However, in contrast to Split, they were always, first and foremost, cities or towns.

In order to achieve the result that the transformation of Diocletian's Palace accomplished organically, we should move toward policy that supports regulation and design in a way that the inadvertence described in the story of the Palace's evolution becomes more purposeful, enabling sustainable reuse on a broader scale. Examples include zoning and building code provisions that anticipate land assembly rather than property-by-property approaches, allow for convertible uses in buildings, provide for a robust mixture of old and new materials, and recognize that both public and private spaces can realize new uses over time, with only minor reconfiguration. Lenders, often the true drivers of development, need to be educated so that they understand the benefits of such reactivated places.

Indeed, some states and cities even have policies encouraging the concept of adaptive reuse. For instance, Los Angeles has a well-established adaptive reuse ordinance[25] that encourages live–work revitalization in certain areas of the city, which has been instrumental to several redevelopment projects.

In addition, a hometown case in point also recently reminded me why we should think beyond limited geographies, time frames, and lifetimes when we discuss urban redevelopment options.

In 2012, the National Trust for Historic Preservation's Seattle-based Preservation Green Lab[26] issued its first report on the environmental benefits of green retrofits applied to historic buildings, as compared to new, state-of-the-art, energy-efficient construction. In one example, a local church that was restored and made into townhouses joined the list of intriguing Seattle adaptive reuse projects typical of national trends. Successive Green Lab "ReUrbanism" reports continue a quantitative approach to preservation and reuse advocacy, as summarized in National Trust president and CEO Stephanie Meeks's recent book, *The Past and Future City*.[27]

Figure 3-24: Seattle: lived a good life.

In one example of ongoing change in rapidly growing Seattle, *Seattle Times* columnist Nicole Brodeur described a protest-free goodbye to a historic neighborhood icon in my Seattle neighborhood (the same neighborhood of the ice cream laundromat and alley movie night—also profiled in chapter 2 and this chapter, respectively); a 112-year-old repair garage and offices were demolished in favor of the nostalgically named "Pike Station," consisting of new, live–work townhouses, complete with a courtyard and intermixed retail.[28]

The purported upshot of the local story missed the relationship to the surrounding city and focused on the single building. Brodeur reported that the building had lived a good life and should yield to a commendable new use—as her headline clearly states, "Sometimes It's OK to Let an Old Landmark Go."

Figures 3-25 and 3-25A: Seattle: Pike Station looms, before and after.

While these recent examples show that not all buildings are alike, and best practices can make a better place, none tell the more holistic, inspirational story of Split, and how human settlements, as a whole, adapt to a changing environment.

Vignette 6: Experiencing the Success of Perception

It should be no surprise that at least one vignette would examine the most fundamental urbanism without effort that is measurable by human response to an urban place rather than by numbers. Sometimes, as in Lisbon, color and quality of light set a tone that seems to defy time and merge with the physical reflection of the city's history—once the center of the Portuguese Empire, and legibly rebuilt from the earthquake of 1755.

Two other examples follow, one evolutionary in the organic sense discussed here, and the other resulting from a mixture of factors in the way an American city has redeveloped at a much-admired scale. From the Cinque Terre towns in Italy and the center of Portland, Oregon, we can see the innate relationships discussed in chapter 2 at work.

Perceiving the Essence of Urbanism

Today's populist urbanism celebrates the rise of the city, whether by census or through science. Along the way, some note a more personal, humanist nostalgia when, for instance, a long-time mom-and-pop store closes, or a formerly distinct urban place merges with conventions from elsewhere, or, perhaps, anywhere.[29] As I have said, our personal observations, feelings, and perceptions can contribute to the urbanism we seek—and, as to urban settlements it is key to reflect when we simply like what we see.

It is exciting when purposefully preserved fragments of the past resonate with a viewer of the present. Such instances occur

Figures 3-26 and 3-26A: Lisbon: light on the street.

Figure 3-27: Manarola: framing the Cinque Terre perception.

more in places like Matera or Split rather than in reconstructed "museum towns," such as Colonial Williamsburg or Sturbridge, or Stockholm's Skansen—it is the *gestalt* of these authentic, historic cities that strikes us and takes us back to a sustainable set of circumstances. We want to live there for a year rather than a day, or to bring the places home—all in the spirit of local sustainable principles referenced by the Baltic Sea Project's discussion of Matera.

In the Cinque Terre, along the coast of northwest Italy, there are five neighborhoods, all self-contained but symbiotic microeconomies connected by footpath, rail, trail, and water. They all have the enviable amenities of street, square, and housing, as well as terraced agriculture and spiritual retreats in the near hinterlands. The Cinque Terre towns of today have evolved as a designated UNESCO World Heritage Site[30] and a national park with regulatory mechanisms to preserve and protect the cultural landscape (including often-abandoned hillside vineyards) and the internationally noted "look and feel" of interconnected towns.[31]

Figure 3-28: Monterosso and the Cinque Terre towns.

Moving forward, these regional artifacts raise a real question: need such places be facade-based shells that are largely touristic—dominated in the summer by strangers who rejoice not just in local wine and pesto, but, ironically, the lack of cars and the wonders of a small-scale, interurban trek?

Can the "we like what we see" elements be the stuff of daily life rather than experienced only on a vacation? Over and above summer jaunts—including shipping home wine and pesto to remember and share—we should all bring home the gift of urban ideas in a way that honors experience, feelings, and perception of the effortless. This gift honors not only the rising tide of urbanist ideas but also the spirit of implementation.

Perceiving a Modern Place

Visits to other cities can easily create "grass is always greener" responses, which are hardly complete analyses of a place. Yet these human, spontaneous gestalts are also worth noting, because they are a response to the immediate look and feel of a location and constitute authentic perceptions of the best of urbanism, not unlike Matera and Split.

In Portland, Oregon, I once presented the results of my coauthored study on transit-oriented and urban center development to a meeting of the American Bar Association's State and Local Government Law Section, and then I co-led a bus tour on specific, local examples in the Lloyd and Pearl Districts and beyond. In keeping with the spirit of gestalt, something very human happened along the way; I realized that, while the reconstituted Portland fabric resulted from a purposeful approach, it felt as effortless as many of the examples I have referenced and used as examples in this book.

Portland's advanced transportation system (including light rail, streetcar, and bicycle) has inspired several urbanist writers, due to

Figure 3-29: Portland: the look and feel of the Pearl District.

its highly walkable downtown and development practices that captured the imagination of a new generation of city-oriented populists. In particular, William Fulton's "six key lesson" summary of Portland's attributes provides useful insights about, inter alia, its "raw material," walkable venues, informality, development, and transportation relationships.[32]

From a fundamental "read the city" perspective, downtown Portland and its close-in neighborhoods capture the best of an urban experience: the scale, street surfaces, and sidewalk furnishings occur amid integrated yet appropriately separated transportation modes and supportive green spaces. Innovative business and community groups have leveraged proximity to transit and managed parking using successful development strategies.

All lead back to tension between the prescriptive approach versus the naturally occurring urbanism identified in the introduction, and to a universal question: *How can we capture this experience in my city?* Perhaps such a fundamental human response is the best metric of all, and the key to achieving a livable place.

Chapter 4

Lessons Learned, Collecting the Diaries

As the last vignette makes clear, perception and feeling are key to understanding and advancing the human relationship with built surroundings. On that note, some years ago I asked a writer friend about how she had expressed her effortless relationship with New York City during the time she lived there. Annie Q. Syed, a talented teacher and former lawyer-turned-writer, offered some particular place-based prose, her remarkable rejoinder to the classic E. B. White essay "Here Is New York." In her own piece, simply entitled "NYC,"[1] Syed begins with the compelling sentence, "New York City is an impractical, yet awe-inspiring, relationship you cannot quit." Syed's response had no small role in furthering my thought processes about the role of figurative, memory-based, and tangible urban diaries, the refinement of the many innate relationships described in chapter 2, and, most particularly, the definition and potential of urbanism without effort.

Questions remain as to how to make the rich backstory of naturally occurring urbanism something that can be marshaled and used as more than humanistic reflection on familiar and comfortable urban settings. In response, this chapter considers how best to weave together the urban diaries urged here, and suggests—for further analysis and application—a cohesive summary approach to the observations set out in chapters 1 through 3.

The Media as Interconnected Diaries

Urbanism without effort can be communicated simply and democratically, with a premium on the impressionistic as much as the analytical. Cities and urban ideas are increasingly touted in conventional media and in online editions, for mainstream readers as well as those who focus on urban topics. The instantaneous, global connections made possible by online urban-oriented publications such as *CityLab*, *Next City*, *Guardian Cities*, and *CityMetric* immediately display that the urban vernacular can be simultaneously multicultural and timeless, or further expressed in the interests of social justice and empowerment, or with emphasis on technological or environmental ends. In each case, through links to multimedia sources, the two dimensions of print can easily become sight, motion, and sound.

For instance, in 2010 Seth Sherwood described the effortless magic of Damascus prior to the Syrian Civil War:

> Damascus loves to flaunt its age. It claims to be *the world's oldest inhabited city*—replete with biblical and Koranic lore, Roman ruins, ancient Islamic edifices and Ottoman-era palaces. But that's not to say the Syrian capital is stuck in time. Dozens of centuries-old mansions have been reborn as Mideast-chic hotels, and fashionable shops and restaurants have arisen in the ancient lanes of the Old City. *Throw in a fledgling generation of bars and clubs, and the age-old metropolis has never looked so fresh* [emphasis added].[2]

In 2013 Andreas Dalsgaard's film *Human Scale* took human nature and the work of Jan Gehl and others to the big screen.[3] The film explained how the traditional human-scale city could reemerge in the modern urban form if expressed as implementable standards that city builders could understand and adapt to building and infrastructure design. While few would describe the profiled megacity success stories as "effortless" in themselves, Dalsgaard's medium became a clear portrayal of how some have attempted to reclaim the intrinsic comfort and scale of naturally occurring urban settings.

In addition, Twitter can still communicate the effortless over and above its now-amplified political tone. The digital age has amplified the art of efficient consumption. To sell today's message of the critical relationship of land use and transportation, jobs close to home, and multimodal forms of transit, references to the principles discussed here can blend with the quest to communicate urbanist messages with a populist voice.

Sarah Marder's Cortona, Italy: A Diary on the World Stage

While the ready availability of YouTube, Vimeo, and other online sites has also allowed for ready communication, film media, such as *The Human Scale*, and similar documentary approaches can provide large-scale urban diaries for mass audiences on a world stage.[4] In particular, American expatriate and film producer Sarah Marder's independent film[5] *The Genius of a Place* addresses universal questions about the dynamics of place in Cortona, Italy, and provides lessons for evolving cities, towns, and neighborhoods everywhere.

Marder, working through her film, offers a useful examination of whether effortless urbanism lost to rapid change can ever be reclaimed. The film summarizes over 25 years of observing a commercial transformation from a tradition-based, agrarian economy to dependence on tourism and world renown after publication of Frances Mayes's *Under the Tuscan Sun*.[6] The film's title is no accident, echoing English poet Alexander Pope's exhortation that we "consult the genius of the place in all." The film crew followed suit, listening to evidence from the Etruscan past to today.

Marder, in partnership with the production company, OLO creative farm, has a broad, international focus premised on history and human nature. "We see Cortona as a symbol for places all around the world facing similar challenges, undergoing rapid change, growth, and construction, and struggling to find a balance between development and conservation." In the footage that her team collected, the clear message is one of a changed commercial fabric, with stores in the historic center now catering almost exclusively to touristic whims rather than residents' needs. It also shows familiar urban challenges, but in Cortona style: like many tourist destinations, real estate prices are increasingly unaffordable for longtime residents, causing relocation to outlying areas; parking availability is often limited; in peak seasons, trash piles grow next to dumpsters; and a well digger explains the need for increased well depths based on substantially increased water demand (as late as the 1950s, Cortona residents were still using 2,000-year-old Etruscan wells scattered throughout the town).

Figure 4-1: The genius of the old ways, near Cortona in the 1950s. (Credit: Professor Duilio Peruzzi)

From my perspective, in bridging common urban-growth experiences worldwide, Marder's endeavor is both remarkable and sincere. What happens to an authentic place forever altered by unexpected notoriety, such as Mayes's arrival, books, and films? How is tradition changed and culture compromised? How should growth be managed and a sustainable local economy preserved? These are not casual questions about the impacts of tourism, but rather about best practices going forward, based on legacies potentially lost.[7]

In fact, places like Cortona, with special topography, viewpoints, and strategic advantage, have long driven human settlement. Cortona was founded by Etruscans nearly 3,000 years ago. Etruscan choice of city location was typically a matter of utmost importance, carried out by specialized elders who knew how to apply the right

Figure 4-2: An ancient borgo, *or tiny village, in Cortona's surrounding countryside.*

criteria for a suitable site. Similar to the Matera and Cinque Terre narratives in chapter 3, such historic hill town settings are instructive for more than romantic vacation ambience—they contain important lessons about successful human settlement.[8]

Time-honored traditions under threat of compromise or extinction is an important paradigm to the ongoing communication of urbanism without effort. *The Genius of a Place* could offer an enviable case study. Between its examination of Cortona's celebrity status and its dozens of thoughtful interviews, the film offers significant insight about placemaking in a global economy.

Perhaps not surprisingly, Marder is routinely pressed to generate "some policy, law, or methodology," something she says that she "is in no place to do." However, she has bigger plans that mirror the best of neighborhood outreach, visioning, and charrette. She hopes that the film—her version of an urban diary—will become a tool for promoting "local stewardship on a global level." Perhaps it will even act as a catalyst for touring workshops, engaging viewers on the unintended consequences of development in their own town or city.

Marder's effort provides discernment of the underlying innate relationships and urbanism without effort at play in one town. The approach is refreshingly aimed at understanding baselines, not dictating results. As an alternative to more directed public life studies, growth management approaches, legislative hearings, and city council deliberations, *The Genius of a Place* merits a careful review.

Ongoing Diaries

The most important factor in understanding the role of inspiration, historical context, and the space-based cues inherent in cities, I conclude, is the content of the urban diaries we amass in the sum total of our urban experience. The diaries document innate relationships as set out in chapter 2, record our experiences, and inform our preferences of place—often based on feeling and perception—as described in the vignettes of chapter 3 and the applied lessons of *Seeing the Better City*. As noted, some urban diaries may remain figurative or internal, while others may appear tangibly in forms of media ranging from tweets to Dalsgaard's and Marder's films.

Whatever the form, they are ongoing, and can reflect the confluence of the effortless and the prescriptive as our ideas of the city alter and emerge.

Next Steps: A Five-Part Inquiry

Are there possibilities to take forward, in a cohesive summary, all that I have presented in this book? Are there ways to further my opening call for a "clean, multidisciplinary slate for reinvigorating the way we think about urban development today"? As a precept to the more applied approach to visual urban diaries carried forward in *Seeing the Better City*, I propose a five-part inquiry as an outline for those who want to attempt meaningful implementation in the context of their own community.

The five-part inquiry proceeds in the manner this book has moved, from diary to contextual understanding to an adaptability analysis under local conditions, followed by a more practical audit of available policy avenues and implementation possibilities. As set out in chapters 2 and 3, even when we have ready examples of naturally occurring urbanism at hand, we are still learning how to address the inherent tension between a prescribed approach and embracing change that occurs more organically. Here is a progression for consideration.

1. Illustration and inspiration—An initial determination of whether the example resonates in a way that can be captured with photos, sketching,[9] or a narrative to provide inspiration for today's adaptation or innovation.
2. Consensus and understanding—Does the example provide a basis for a ground-up rather than a top-down administration, thereby allowing for each individual to more readily understand his or her neighborhood or city?

3. Can the example work locally?—Does local context (factors such as culture, climate, topography, political structure) allow for integration of the original example with local policy or regulatory goals?
4. Necessity/baselines for policy, planning, and regulatory reform—If necessary, can the example translate to a policy, planning, or regulatory reform initiative?
5. Implementation—What further actions would be necessary on behalf of government or private-sector stakeholders to implement the example on a broader basis while avoiding an overly prescriptive approach?

Closing

WE ARE NOT THE FIRST IN HISTORY to attempt a reorientation of how cities work, nor will we be the last. Today, technology companies play an increasing role in "smart city" design.[1] "Smart growth" debates address urban automobile dominance, and the consequences of driverless vehicles. A few years ago, science fiction presented apt analogies. From 2003 to 2009, the remake of the 1970s television space opera *Battlestar Galactica* dramatically examined the ambiguous relationship between human, nature, and machine.

Consider the useful lessons from *Battlestar Galactica*'s conjectural future, which profiles the battle of the arch-enemy human against the rebel Cylon machine, both ironically searching for a framework for a better tomorrow. To quote a Cylon or two, "This has all happened before. And it will happen again."

Today's urban stakeholders continue the quest to redefine, or "optimize," cities based on the relationship between transportation and land use, and renewed sensitivity to affordable housing and climate change.[2] Yet many of the issues surrounding today's cities are universal and timeless, no matter how they are labeled or described. When we discuss urban transportation choices, the role of nature in the city, housing affordability, and aesthetics, we often rush to recreate successes from elsewhere, without first acknowledging and recalling imagery of the most latent or "effortless" examples.

We remain at a literal and figurative crossroads in this quest. During this book's gestation, from 2009 until republication today, several cities around the world were spontaneously transformed by the uncertainty of the many forces that shape city life—from social uprisings to hurricanes, military occupations to gun and terrorist violence—as well as economic challenges. In many cases, outcomes suddenly and dramatically transformed urban places, from Damascus to towns on the Jersey Shore to Newtown, Connecticut, and Parkland, Florida, to Paris, London, Nice, and many more.

In the meantime, light rail and streetcars, new city plans, regulations, parks, smart city dashboards, and neighborhood activism forge on. Their advocates are implementing ideal, efficient approaches to city development and operation, which sometimes underemphasize the multidisciplinary, ecumenical nature of the city, and the latent, unpredictable aspects of everyday city life. On one day we might champion the sustainable, open space or bicycle initiatives of Barcelona or Copenhagen, on the next the remaking of Times Square in New York City, or affordability solutions in London, San Francisco, or Seattle. But all in all, today's quest for sustainable urban forms are static snapshots, multiplied and confounded by the rampant messaging of our digital age.

As a lawyer and consultant, I've seen the risks of advocating how others should live without consideration of local needs, or a sustainable authenticity built on applicable history and context. Rather than spur only objection and opposition, we must find sympathetic ways to address resistance to change and implementation. Here, my purpose is to offer a straightforward return to first principles as the baseline for my companion book, *Seeing the Better City*, and related inquiries into urban observation, context, and authenticity. We should borrow wisely from the anachronistic and basic—and embrace and champion instances of effortless urbanism.

Notes

Introduction

1. For more about Steven Wright quotations, see https://www.goodreads.com/quotes/5305-right-now-i-m-having-amnesia-and-d-j-vu-at-the.

2. Christopher Alexander, "A City Is Not a Tree," *Architectural Forum* 122 (April 1965), 58–62.

3. See Richard Greenwald, "Why Is Authenticity So Central to Urban Culture?" *CityLab*, January 31, 2013, https://www.citylab.com/design/2013/01/why-authenticity-so-central-urban-culture/4543/.

4. For information about "Pavement to Parks," see http://pavementtoparks.org.

5. See Jeff Risom and Mayra Madriz, "Embracing the Paradox of Planning for Informality," *Next City*, January 1, 2018, https://nextcity.org/features/view/embracing-the-paradox-of-planning-for-informality.

6. See Rob Goodspeed's blog entry, "The Relevance and Irrelevance of Richard Sennett," November 29, 2007, http://goodspeedupdate.com/2007/2162.

7. See Daniel Chatman's work summarized by Eric Jaffe, "'Transit' May Not Be Essential to Transit-Oriented Development," *CityLab*, June 10, 2013, https://www.citylab.com/equity/2013/06/transit-might-not-be-essential-transit-oriented-development/5851/.

8. Regional Plan Association, *Regional Plan of New York and Its Environs* (New York: The Regional Plan Association, 1929).

9. Memorandum, Adams to Perry, January 23, 1928, *Papers*, Regional Plan Association, Cornell University.

10. See Trent Noll, "Placemaking: Practices Evolve, Basics Remain," *Planetizen*, December 2, 2010, https://www.planetizen.com/node/47096.

Chapter 1

1. For a dictionary definition of urbanism, see https://www.merriam-webster.com/dictionary/urbanism.

2. "Desire lines" are one way to understand this organic flow. See Robert Moor, "Tracing (and Erasing) New York's Lines of Desire," *The New Yorker*, February 20, 2017, https://www.newyorker.com/tech/elements/tracing-and-erasing-new-yorks-lines-of-desire.

3. For an example of a purposeful approach, see Mike Lydon and Anthony Garcia, *Tactical Urbanism: Short-Term Action for Long-Term Change* (Washington, DC: Island Press, 2015).

4. See Alison Arieff, "It's Time to Rethink 'Temporary,'" *New York Times*, December 19, 2011, https://opinionator.blogs.nytimes.com/2011/12/19/its-time-to-rethink-temporary/.

5. Read more about Walk Score at https://www.walkscore.com.

6. Read more about the Australian placemaking tool, Place Score, at http://www.placescore.org.

7. Read more about the London-based tool to measure urban form characteristics at https://grist.org/article/2010-06-21-measuring-neighborhood-diversity-and-liveliness-with-janescore/.

8. See Jonathan Hiskes, "Measuring neighborhood diversity and liveliness with 'JaneScore,'" *Grist*, June 22, 2010, https://grist.org/article/2010-06-21-measuring-neighborhood-diversity-and-liveliness-with-janescore/.

9. For Steve Mouzon's proposed WalkAppeal classification approach, see http://www.originalgreen.org/blog/walk-appeal.html?fb_comment_id=fbc_10150916012636891_22379968_10150941931091891#f12adfe3e51721e.

10. Joseph Rykwert, *The Idea of a Town: The Anthropology of Urban Form in Rome, Italy and the Ancient World* (Princeton: Princeton University Press, 1976), 24. See also characterization of the city as artifact by Sir John Summerson, Anthony N. B. Garvan, and Christopher Tunnard in Oscar Handlin and John Ely Burchard, eds., *The Historian and the City* (Cambridge: M.I.T. Press, 1963).

11. Tony Hiss, *The Experience of Place* (New York: Vintage Books, 1991), 99.

12. Charles R. Wolfe, *Seeing the Better City* (Washington, DC: Island Press, 2015).

13. Alexander Cockburn, "Bwana Vistas," *Harper's Magazine*, August 1985, 65–69.

14. See Charles R. Wolfe, "Remembrance of Cities Past: Spectacular Photos of the Way We Lived," *Grist*, June 29, 2011, http://grist.org/cities/2011-06-28-the-continued-relevance-of-reclaiming-the-urban-memory/, quoting Burton Holmes in Seoul, Korea, 1899, courtesy of his biographer, Genoa Caldwell.

15. W. Lloyd Warner and others, *Yankee City*, abridged edition (New Haven: Yale University Press, 1975).

16. Robert S. Lynd and Helen M. Lynd, *Middletown: A Study in Contemporary American Culture* (New York: Harcourt, Brace, and Company, 1929).

17. M. R. Wolfe, "A Visual Supplement to Urban Social Studies," *Journal of the American Institute of Planners* 31, no. 1 (February 1965), 51–62.

18. Charles R. Wolfe, *Seeing the Better City*.

19. Ada Louise Huxtable, "Living with the Fake and Liking It," *New York Times*, March 30, 1997, http://www.nytimes.com/1997/03/30/arts/living-with-the-fake-and-liking-it.html. Huxtable's obituary appears at http://www.nytimes.com/2013/01/09/arts/design/ada-louise-huxtable-appraisal-of-an-architecture-critic.html?_r=0.

20. Ibid.

21. See Chuck Wolfe, "Walkable cities, so how come pedestrian malls usually fail?" *Crosscut*, September 24, 2009, https://crosscut.com/2009/09/walkable-cities-so-how-come-pedestrian-malls-usual.

22. For documentary films on Arlington's successful smart growth and transit-oriented development strategies, see https://tv.arlingtonva.us/smart-growth/.

23. For King Lear's famous quotation, in Act I of the play, "Nothing will come of nothing; speak again," see http://shakespeare.mit.edu/lear/lear.1.1.html.

24. Grady Clay, *Close-Up: How to Read the American City* (Chicago: University of Chicago Press, 1980), 11.

25. See Richard Reep, "New Urbanism's Economic Athlete's Heel," *New Geography*, October 30, 2008, http://www.newgeography.com/content/00370-new-urbanism's-economic-achilles-heel.

26. See Erin Chantry, "The New, New Urbanism," *At the Helm of the Public Realm* (blog), January 27, 2013, https://helmofthepublicrealm.com/2013/01/27/the-new-new-urbanism/.

27. See Vladimir Gintoff, "12 Projects That Explain Landscape Urbanism and How It's Changing the Face of Cities," *ArchDaily*, April 6, 2016, https://www.archdaily.com/784842/12-projects-that-show-how-landscape-urbanism-is-changing-the-face-of-cities.

28. For background on low impact development, see the U.S. Environmental Protection Agency's green infrastructure webpage at https://www.epa.gov/green-infrastructure.

29. For an example of Melbourne's programmed outdoor cinema events, see https://whatson.melbourne.vic.gov.au/Whatson/Films/SpecialEvents/Pages/c5b956c8-a4b6-4903-9f63-7068b808ab26.aspx.

30. For the Jewish Virtual Library's brief history of the Venetian Ghetto, see http://www.jewishvirtuallibrary.org/venice-italy-jewish-history-tour.

31. Emily Talen, *City Rules: How Regulations Affect Urban Form* (Washington, DC: Island Press, 2013).

32. René Dubos, *Man Adapting* (New Haven: Yale University Press, 1965).

33. René Dubos, *So Human an Animal* (New York: Scribner's Sons, 1968).

34. For UNESCO's summary of the "*Trulli* of Alberobello," see http://whc.unesco.org/en/list/787.

35. Roberta Brandes Gratzs, *The Living City* (New York: Simon and Schuster, 1989).

36. Joseph Rykwert, *The Seduction of Place: The History and Future of Cities* (New York: Vintage Books, 2002).

37. Download the Urban Land Institute's 2011 "What's Next?" report at http://americas.uli.org/wp-content/uploads/sites/125/ULI-Documents/WhatsNext.pdf.

38. Joseph Rykwert, *The Seduction of Place*, 8.

39. Lewis Mumford, *The City in History* (New York: Harcourt, Brace & World, Inc., 1961).

40. Ibid.

41. J. B. Jackson, "The Discovery of the Street," in *The Necessity for Ruins, and Other Topics* (Amherst, MA: University of Massachusetts Press, 1980), 55.

42. Ibid. According to Jackson, likely writing in the 1970s, the symbol of the modern city is a collection of streets as seen from above, a mere "cartographic abstraction" of implied richness, because the bird's-eye relationship between public byways and private space is how we now understand urban areas. In contrast, Jackson described the foundational and compact vertical city of towers amid a landscape perceived by the medieval resident of long ago—who did not need to understand public streets and spaces—while living a straightforward human- and animal-propelled life of short journeys to work, church, market, and neighbors.

43. Jan Gehl, *Cities for People* (Washington, DC: Island Press, 2010).

44. Rem Koolhaas, "The Generic City," in Rem Koolhaas and Bruce Mau, *S,M,L,XL* (New York: Monacelli Press, 1995).

45. John Kaliski, "The Present City and the Practice of City Design," in John Chase, Margaret Crawford, and John Kaliski, *Everyday Urbanism: Featuring John Chase* (New York: Monacelli Press, 1999), 106. In 1951, Jackson penned similar words:

> [I]t strikes me that some of our planners need to acquire a more robust idea of city life. Perhaps I do them an injustice, but I often have the feeling that their emphasis on convenience, cleanliness, and safety, their distrust of everything vulgar and small and poor is symptomatic of a very lopsided view of urban culture.

J. B. Jackson, "The Stranger's Path," in *Landscapes, Selected Writings of J.B. Jackson*, ed. Ervin H. Zube (Amherst: University of Massachusetts Press, 1970), 105.

Chapter 2

1. Similar questions are no doubt at the root of any analysis of urban development, including more classic twentieth-century inquiries, ranging from Le Corbusier's stark modernist approach to the organic, bustling urbanism described by Jane Jacobs in *The Death and Life of Great American Cities* (New York: Vintage Books, 1961). The seminal works of Lewis Mumford, Christopher Alexander, Kevin Lynch, and William H. Whyte also examined the role of urban form and order from academic, design, and planning perspectives.

2. Joseph Rykwert, *The Idea of a Town: The Anthropology of Urban Form in Rome, Italy and the Ancient World* (Princeton: Princeton University Press, 1976), conclusion.

3. John R. Stilgoe, *Outside Lies Magic: Regaining History and Awareness in Everyday Places* (New York: Walker and Co., 1998).

4. Grady Clay, *Close-Up: How to Read the American City* (Chicago: University of Chicago Press, 1980), 11.

5. Tony Hiss, The *Experience of Place* (New York: Vintage Books, 1991).

6. For instance, various websites active during writing and revision of this book celebrate the possibilities for narrow streets in Los Angeles, alleys in Seattle, walkability in Dallas, and the legacy of Jane Jacobs's urban spaces. In particular, small-scale multimedia producers, such as Streetfilms, document and celebrate notable examples—usually cities of inspiration from around the world.

7. In Seattle, city engineer Dongho Chang is well known for his daily tweets and Instagram posts about ongoing improvements to Seattle's bicycle and pedestrian infrastructure.

8. See Kasey Klimes, "The Real Reason Why Bicycles Are the Key to Better Cities," *Next City*, May 18, 2011, https://nextcity.org/daily/entry/the-real-reason-why-bicycles-are-the-key-to-better-cities.

9. I previously termed this effort an "urban audit," oriented around several questions addressing quality of life issues. See Charles R. Wolfe, "'Getting There, Going There and Almost There': An Audit for Urbanists," *myurbanist* (blog), January 30, 2011, http://www.myurbanist.com/archives/5620.

10. See also my original post on urban diaries: "Creating the Urban Diary," *myurbanist* (blog), June 4, 2011, http://www.myurbanist.com/archives/6397. Specifically, I offer five suggestions for framing surroundings:

1. On your next walk from where you live to a destination of choice, summarize the experience in one paragraph.
2. Take five photos of your favorite neighborhood locations.
3. Think about somewhere you wish was closer to where you live. Pick an ideal location, and write about or photograph how you would travel from here to there.
4. Videotape a walk, bike ride, or roadside activity along a street.
5. Using burst or continuous mode on a camera, photograph street life that you observe from a passenger window.

11. Ibid.

12. For further information on the Brundtland Report, see UN World Commission on Environment and Development, "Our Common Future," 1987. http://www.un-documents.net/wced-ocf.htm.

13. Ibid.

14. For an informative video summary of Busquets's hypothesis, see https://player.vimeo.com/video/19659471.

15. Edmund N. Bacon, *Design of Cities*, rev. ed. (Middlesex, UK: Penguin Books, 1978).

16. For Forterra's summary of its Landscape Construction and Local Infrastructure Program (LCLIP), see https://forterra.org/service/lclip-landscape-conservation-and-local-infrastructure-program.

17. Lewis Mumford, "What Is a City?" *Architectural Record*, 82 (November 1937), 185.

18. J. B. Jackson, "The Necessity for Ruins," in *The Necessity for Ruins, and Other Topics* (Amherst, MA: University of Massachusetts Press, 1980), 89.

19. Albert Camus, *The Myth of Sisyphus and Other Essays*, Justin O'Brien trans. (New York: Vintage Books, 1991).

20. Elliot Liebow, *Tally's Corner: A Study of Negro Streetcorner Men* (Boston: Little, Brown and Company, 1967).

21. For details on the Laundromat Café, see https://www.thelaundromatcafe.com/en/home.

22. For more on Brain Wash, see http://www.brainwash.com.

23. See Charles R. Wolfe, "The Quest to Make Regulatory Reform Work in Seattle," *CityLab*, March 27, 2012, https://www.citylab.com/equity/2012/03/quest-make-regulatory-reform-work-seattle/1607/.

24. Rupert Brooke, *Letters from America* (1916; rev. ed., London: Hesperus, 2007), ch. 3.

25. See Feargus O'Sullivan, "A 'Night Mayor Is Transforming Amsterdam after Dark," *CityLab*, January 29, 2016, https://www.citylab.com/solutions/2016/01/night-mayor-amsterdam-mirik-milan/433893/.

26. For a commendable summary of studies of cities at night, see the MIT syllabus at http://www.mit.edu/~susannes/pdf_files/World-of-Night-9-15a.pdf.

27. For details on the International CPTED Organization, see http://www.cpted.net.

28. See Tim Halibur, "Women, Transit and the Perception of Safety," *Planetizen*, February 27, 2010, https://www.planetizen.com/node/42878. See also Jana Korn, "Women's Safety Must Be a Part of Transportation Planning," *Next City*, March 27, 2018, https://nextcity.org/daily/entry/womens-safety-must-be-part-of-transportation-planning.

29. For resources compiled for Seattle-area communities by the Puget Sound Regional Council, see https://www.psrc.org/sites/default/files/crime_prevention_through_environmental_design.pdf.

30. For a helpful summary of the Rockville, Maryland, guidelines, see https://www.rockvillemd.gov/documentcenter/view/938.

31. See Charles R. Wolfe, "The Quest to Make Regulatory Reform Work in Seattle."

Chapter 3

1. Borrowing from Professor Margaret O'Mara's cautionary tale about attempts to replicate the success of Silicon Valley around the world. See Margaret O'Mara, "Don't Try This at Home," *Foreign Policy*, September/October 2010. For an August 6, 2010, online version, see http://foreignpolicy.com/2010/08/06/dont-try-this-at-home/.

2. For more information on the Laetoli Track and footprints, see http://www.pbs.org/wgbh/evolution/library/07/1/l_071_03.html.

3. Richard Jackson, *Designing Healthy* Communities (San Francisco: Jossey-Bass, 2012).

4. See Diane Hales, "An Italian Tradition: La Passeggiata," http://www.fodors.com/news/story_4117.html, describing observations in Giovanna P. Delnegro, *The Passeggiata and Popular Culture in an Italian Town: Folklore and the Performance of Modernity* (Montreal: McGill-Queen's University Press, 2004).

5. For the Project for Public Spaces' summary of Las Ramblas's attributes, see https://www.pps.org/places/las-ramblas.

6. For more context on the Campo de' Fiori, see http://www.aviewoncities.com/rome/campodeifiori.htm.

7. For *myurbanist* (blog) video clips of night activity in the Piazza Navona, see http://www.myurbanist.com/archives/464.

8. See Charles R. Wolfe, "Making Big Urban Ideas Happen through Idea Management, *The Huffington Post*, May 27, 2011, http://www.huffingtonpost.com/charles-r-wolfe/making-big-urban-ideas-ha_b_867277.html.

9. See Alyse Nelson, "Alley Alley, In Come Free," *Sightline* (blog), August 27, 2011, http://www.sightline.org/2011/08/26/alley-alley-in-come-free-2/ (updated with July 2016 editorial link to *CityLab*), https://www.citylab.com/solutions/2016/07/a-new-life-for-urban-alleys/491207/?utm_source=Sightline+Institute&utm_medium=web-email&utm_campaign=Sightline+News+Selections).

10. For more information on Daniel Toole's book, see http://www.blurb.com/b/2319461-tight-urbanism?ce=blurb_ew&utm_source=widget.

11. Listen to the March 18, 2010, KUOW radio production, "Rethinking Our Alleys," at http://www2.kuow.org/program.php?id=19734.

12. For additional resources on the Ngorongoro Conservation Area, see http://www.ngorongorocrater.org.

13. For a brief profile of the Maasai of Tanzania, see http://www.kitumusote.org/history.

14. Chuck Mahron, "A Brief Look Back," *Strong Towns* (blog), March 29, 2011, https://www.strongtowns.org/journal/2011/3/29/a-brief-look-back.html.

15. For more information on the Matera World Heritage Site, see http://whc.unesco.org/en/list/670.

16. Carlo Levi, *Christ Stopped at Eboli: The Story of a Year* (New York: Farrar, Strauss and Company, 1947).

17. See and download UNESCO, The Baltic Sea Project, Learners' Guide 8, "Observing and Innovating Urban Ecology in the Baltic Sea Region," p. 18, www.b-s-p.org/upload/guides/lg8.pdf.

18. For more information on the Split/Palace of Diocletian World Heritage Site, see http://whc.unesco.org/en/list/97.

19. See Thomas Swick, "Croatian Pop," *South Florida SunSentinel*. November 26, 2000, http://articles.sun-sentinel.com/2000-11-26/travel/0011170954_1_stone-room-houses.

20. For online views of Robert Adam's drawings, see http://digicoll.library.wisc.edu/cgi-bin/DLDecArts/DLDecArts-idx?id=DLDecArts.AdamRuins.

21. Jerko Marasović and Tomislav Marasović, *Diocletian Palace* (Split, Croatia: Zora, 1968).

22. See Barbara Noe, "In Diocletian's Living Room," *National Geographic Intelligent Travel* (blog), March 6, 2015, http://intelligenttravel.nationalgeographic.com/2015/03/05/in-diocletians-living-room/?_ga=2.14621111.1098916732.1520354629-1351182066.1520354629.

23. For the dramatic Panoramic Earth imagery of Split, see https://www.panoramicearth.com/s/diocletian/0.

24. Thomas Swick: "Croatian Pop."

25. Download the exemplary 2006 revised Los Angeles adaptive reuse program manual at https://www.downtownla.com/images/reports/adaptive-rescue-ordinance.pdf.

26. For more on the work of the Preservation Green Lab, see https://savingplaces.org/preservation-green-lab#.Wp7Lv2aZPOQ.

27. Stephanie Meeks, *The Past and Future City: How Historic Preservation Is Reviving America's Communities* (Washington, DC: Island Press, 2016).

28. See Nicole Brodeur, "Sometimes It's OK to Let an Old Landmark Go," *Seattle Times*, January 30, 2012, https://www.seattletimes.com/seattle-news/sometimes-its-ok-to-let-an-old-landmark-go/.

29. For a remarkable essay on a transition from somewhere to anywhere, see Jonathan Raban, "Boomtown USA," *Financial Times*, June 29, 2007, https://www.ft.com/content/ed2fff50-22c4-11dc-ac53-000b5df10621.

30. For more information on the Cinque Terre World Heritage Site, see http://whc.unesco.org/en/list/826.

31. For the comprehensive multilingual national park website, see http://www.parconazionale5terre.it/?id_lingue=2.

32. See William Fulton, "Six Key Lessons from Portland's Urbanism," *Crosscut* (repurposed from *Citiwire*), September 20, 2009, https://crosscut.com/2009/09/six-key-lessons-from-portlands-urbanism.

Chapter 4

1. See Annie Syed's discussion of her poem in her September 2, 2012, blog entry, "A Still Sunday between New York and San Francisco," at http://annieqsyed.com/2012/09/02/a-still-sunday-between-nyc-and-san-francisco/.

2. See Seth Sherwood, "36 Hours in Damascus," *New York Times*, December 1, 2010, http://www.nytimes.com/2010/12/05/travel/05hours.html?pagewanted=all.

3. See *Human Scale*, Official Trailer at http://www.nytimes.com/2010/12/05/travel/05hours.html?pagewanted=all.

4. Gary Hustwit's film *Urbanized* also showed the potential of portraying today's city orientation in a theater setting. See Charles R. Wolfe, "How 'Urbanized' Challenges Us to Make Our Cities Better," *The Atlantic*, September 29, 2011, http://www.theatlantic.com/national/archive/2011/09/how-urbanized-challenges-us-to-make-our-cities-better/245891/.

5. The best summary of Marder's message is through the film's website, www.thegeniusofaplace.com, which contains a final trailer and paid links to view the full version.

6. Frances Mayes, *Under the Tuscan Sun: At Home in Italy* (San Francisco: Chronicle Books, 1996).

7. As Marder explained during our several discussions in 2011–2012, and an in-person meeting in Milan in 2014:

> As I saw things begin to change starting around 2000, I wanted to find a way to document some aspects of Cortona before they changed beyond recognition or repair. I especially wanted to document the way of life of the elderly, which resembles life from centuries ago, because I could see that it would soon be extinct. Ironically, I seemed to be among the few noticing. From the perspective of many, it was a non-issue—most people embraced their day-to-day concerns and were not worried that the town might change in unsatisfactory ways. They took the town's well-being for granted, given the previous and successful navigation of almost 3000 years of history.

8. These settings blend with natural surroundings; keep up a pedestrian identity, with limited vehicular access; emphasize aesthetic principles (views to and from); communally group institutions around public open space; carefully merge public pathways and private dwellings; offer efficient living spaces and allowance for density; as well as display innovative bases for water collection and storage and management of sewage and stormwater discharge.

9. In many cities, sketching advocates and active, well-known individuals (such as Gabriel Campinario in Seattle and Richard Briggs in Sydney) and groups show the potential of the medium to inspire and inform.

Closing

1. Emily Badger, "Tech Envisions the Ultimate Start-Up: An Entire City," *New York Times*, February 24, 2018, https://www.nytimes.com/2018/02/24/upshot/tech-envisions-the-ultimate-start-up-an-entire-city.html.

2. This book's original edition contained a similar proposition. See also Badger, ibid.

About the Author

Charles R. Wolfe provides a unique perspective on cities as a London- and Seattle-based urbanist writer, photographer, land use consultant, and attorney. He is a visiting scholar at KTH University (Royal Institute of Technology) in Stockholm, and a longtime affiliate associate professor in the College of Built Environments at the University of Washington in Seattle, where he teaches land use law at the graduate level. During summer 2018, Wolfe was a Fulbright Specialist under the auspices of the Australian-American Fulbright Commission, based at the Cairns and Townsville campuses of James Cook University. Wolfe is the author of *Seeing the Better City* (Island Press, 2017) and has contributed regularly on urban development topics to several publications, including *CityLab*, *The Atlantic*, *The Huffington Post*, *CityMetric*, *Governing*, and *Planetizen*. He blogs at myurbanist.com.

Acknowledgments for the Revised Edition

Since the original e-book publication of *Urbanism Without Effort* in 2013, my further immersion in international venues and experiences with new friends and colleagues have only enhanced opportunities to acknowledge those important to both the original and the revised editions. I would like to particularly thank once more several people who kindly listened and offered suggestions along the way to *Urbanism Without Effort*. As before, my wife, Fiona de Kerckhove, provided helpful edits with lawyerly precision, encouragement, and a bridge to three continents for inspiration. My brother, Michael Wolfe, explained the architect's view during two trips to Italy and France and reminded me of the context inherent in urban form. Dr. Tigran Haas, director of the Centre for the Future of Places at KTH University (Royal Institute of Technology) in Stockholm, was instrumental in both encouraging and then arranging for the funding of this revision. Still-valuable resources were consulted again, including those assembled by Virginia Werner, a Seattle built environment professional, who, as an M.U.P. and M.L.A. master's degree candidate at the University of Washington, provided research and related assistance in 2012. Thanks also to many supportive editors from 2009 to the present who encouraged content that was later adopted here, most particularly my Island Press editor Courtney Lix, who originally helped shepherd *Urbanism Without Effort* to fruition and was excited to do so again in both hard-copy and e-book forms.

Index

Page numbers followed by "f" indicate figures.

Island Press | Board of Directors